**Roslyn Young** was born in Australia and after obtaining a BA and a Dip. Ed. from the University of Queensland, she taught English literature in Australian schools for a few years.

She moved to France in 1967 and worked at the University of Franche-Comté in the Centre de Linguistique Appliquée from 1968 until she retired, teaching English and sometimes French in intensive courses. She met Gattegno for the first time in 1971 in Geneva, where she saw him teach an hour of Chinese. She knew immediately that she wanted to be able to teach in this way.

Roslyn wrote her doctoral thesis on Gattegno's model and its relevance to his work in language teaching. She has published around 30 articles on teaching and the Silent Way.

Roslyn has worked for the Gattegno association in France, Une Education Pour Demain, since the beginning of the 1980's, and continues to do teacher training for this association. (Teacher training can be anything between a two-day course on a specific subject and a five-year programme designed to produce a new generation of teacher trainers.)


**Piers Messum** studied mathematics and law at Cambridge University before becoming a computer programmer. He taught English in Japan in the mid-1980's where he learnt Japanese in a Silent Way class. He first met Gattegno there, at a seminar where Gattegno described the application of his model to the problem of health.

After working in software sales, Piers started teaching English again in 1991, this time using the Silent Way. He became interested in how pronunciation is learned, and wrote a doctoral thesis at University College London which developed some of Gattegno's ideas to explain how children learn the pronunciation of their first language.

Most recently Piers has been teaching English in London while continuing his academic research.

# How We Learn and How We Should be Taught

An introduction to the work of
Caleb Gattegno

# How We Learn and How We Should be Taught

An introduction to the work of
Caleb Gattegno

Volume 1

Roslyn Young
and
Piers Messum

*Duo Flumina*

First published in 2011 by Duo Flumina Ltd

112 Warner Road, London SE5 9HQ

www.duoflumina.com


ISBN

978 0 9568755 0 1 - paperback

978 0 9568755 1 8 - hardback

Printed in the United Kingdom

# Contents

# Part III  Where do we come from?

# Acknowledgments

We would like to thank all the people who made it possible for Gattegno to give seminars and publish his ideas during his lifetime, and who have promoted his work since his death.

Within this group, we are personally indebted to Fusako Allard, Malik Berkane, David B. Davies, Michael Hollyfield, Suzanne Lachaise, Maurice Laurent, members of the Science of Education reading group within the Association of Teachers of Mathematics, the English teachers at the Centre de Linguistique Appliquée at the University of Franche-Comté in Besançon, the teacher trainers and staff of Une Education Pour Demain, and Educational Solutions Worldwide Inc.

Roslyn Young would also like to thank Christiane Rozet for her unfailing support, Leon Stemler and Eric Lepoint who read earlier versions of this book and made many helpful suggestions, and participants in her seminars who helped her to deepen her understanding through their questions and contributions.

Piers Messum would also like to thank Marie-Laure Lagrange, Richard Starkey and Claire Suthren for their support and for the insights they have brought into conversations about Gattegno and his work.

# Preface

Newton, Maxwell and Einstein are considered to be great scientists because they created syntheses out of observations that until then had been unrelated. Their theories gave us a more coherent understanding of the universe we live in. With the single concept of gravitational attraction, Newton accounted for phenomena as varied as the falling to the ground of an apple, the rise and fall of the tides and the movements of celestial bodies. After Faraday had linked electricity and magnetism, James Clerk Maxwell mathematized their relationship into a unified theory of these and other electromagnetic phenomena including light.

In the field of physics, the nineteenth century also saw a growing awareness that many of the phenomena studied by physicists were in fact different forms of one single entity which they finally called 'energy'.

Caleb Gattegno, who began his career as a mathematician, realised that if he was to explain how humans live their lives, it would be necessary for him to add other distinct forms of energy to those studied by physicists. He set out to identify and systematise these human energies. Einstein had already proposed that the whole of the universe is energy, transformed or not into matter. Gattegno saw that this statement should encompass not only the material world, as Einstein intended, but also the worlds of the biological and human sciences. At the same time, it was clear that we are in a process of evolution, as Darwin had described in *The Evolution of Species*, published in 1859. Gattegno concluded that if both Einstein and Darwin are correct, then energy itself is in a process of evolution. He therefore realised that it would be possible to recast the history of the universe, including all human activity, in terms of the evolution of energy, and worked on this project for the rest of his life.

Thus, he consciously and deliberately placed himself in the tradition of scientists who create syntheses, and gave himself the task of creating a unifying theory which would allow all areas of human endeavour to be understood within a general model of the universe, a model integrating everything known to scientists in the natural, biological and human sciences. According to Gattegno, his model is not only universal but also dynamic, by which he meant that it could be easily modified to take into account newly discovered phenomena. However, he also anticipated that it would be replaced at some time in the future by another, more comprehensive model.

For many years, Gattegno worked in close contact with Jean-Emile Marcault and Thérèse Brosse who had developed an energy-based vision of psychology and medicine (Marcault & Brosse, 1939). Gattegno accepted their proposition that each person is directed by an energy which they had called 'the self'.

Their work also led him to the understanding that human beings have given themselves education as a tool in order to further their evolution. Since, for Gattegno, the whole universe could be understood as energy evolving, with human beings as the latest product of this evolution, he saw that if a genuine understanding of human learning could be developed, then humans would stand on the threshold of a new capacity: they would reach the very motor of their own evolution.

He therefore considered that one of his major contributions was to have created a science of education, based on the study of human energy and energies.

Sciences generate technologies and Gattegno's science of education is no exception. It has generated applications in many fields: Words in Color and Infused Reading for the teaching and learning of reading in any alphabetic language; Numbers in Color, Animated Geometry and Cuisenaire Rods (also known as Algebricks) for the teaching and learning of Mathematics at all levels from kindergarten through to the end of secondary school; and The Silent Way for the teaching and learning of any foreign language, with materials so far developed for more than forty. His ideas have also been successfully applied in History, Geography, Chemistry, Physics and other disciplines.

As can be seen in what follows, in all his work Gattegno gave himself both the obligation of taking into account all factual scientific knowledge to date, and the right to demur from the theories that other scientists have developed from these same facts.

## Notes

1    Drawing Gattegno's ideas together has been a challenge for several reasons.

Firstly, he developed his model over a lifetime, and it evolved.

Secondly, he regularly needed to restate his own ideas because his model is an integrated whole, but applicable in quite diverse domains. He expressed his ideas somewhat differently depending on the main subject of each publication and the weight he needed to give to any part of the model in a particular context.

Thirdly, one important source for us has been his seminars. In these, he was careful to work in such a way that his audience would be able to understand his ideas, with the result that these were not always expressed in their most developed form but were more contextualised than when he wrote on the same subjects in his books. More than twenty of these seminars have been transcribed, most of them in French.

At the same time, on several occasions he stated that when he wrote books and newsletters he did so primarily to express himself accurately and only secondarily to communicate with contemporary readers. He explained that he was content to be writing for readers living in a world 50 years hence. Thus his seminars and his books and newsletters provide significantly different perspectives on his work.

All this has forced us to make choices in what we present. We would welcome any books and articles written by others in which what we have treated is described differently and in which other parts of the model are given more prominence.

2    The first draft of this book emerged from Roslyn Young's doctoral thesis. Piers Messum collaborated with her to produce this revised and enlarged text. The examples that are in the first person come from Roslyn's life unless otherwise indicated.

3    In some places we have used Gattegno's choice of a word or words without direct attribution, partly to avoid interrupting the flow of a text that is not meant to be an academic treatise, but mainly because the whole

book is a presentation of Gattegno's thinking as we have come to understand it and we make no pretence of having been the originators of the ideas expressed. At the end of each chapter we have indicated the major sources for our presentation under the heading 'Further Reading'.

4        For convenience in the use of pronouns, we have decided to speak of female teachers and caregivers and male students and children in the examples we describe.

5        In this volume, we deal mainly with the 'How we learn' part of the title. 'How we should be taught' will be the subject of volume 2.


Gattegno's work was about things that matter. It continues to inspire because people recognise themselves in the detailed descriptions he gave of how it is to live a human life, and through these descriptions they come to know themselves better. If they are teachers, this knowledge can transform the way they work, as they discover the joy it is capable of creating in classrooms. We hope that this book will give others better access to his work.

# Part I

# Who am I? And who are my students?

"I need to start with something I can rely on. Is there anything more primitive than self-awareness?"

Caleb Gattegno - *A Working Model for Health*

# 1 On presence, awareness and awarenesses

## My inner life

As soon as I stop going about my everyday business for a few minutes and look inside myself, I cannot fail to notice that I have an inner life. This inner life is made up of thoughts and memories; emotions and feelings; inner climates; the sensations that I feel inside and what my sense organs put me in contact with from outside; uncertainties, questions and judgments; plans and commitments; ... all the mental activity which is part of living my life.

## Presence and awareness

It is my presence which gives me access to my life, both inner and outer. My presence constantly moves from here to there, allowing me to become aware of whatever is accessible to me within myself and in the environment.

> It is late at night. I stop typing this text for a moment and let myself become present to the world around me. Immediately I hear the cars in the street and other noises from the neighbourhood. I begin typing again but this time, instead of being present to my thoughts as is usual when I write, I deliberately move my presence to my ears. I am immediately struck by the chattering of the keys as they strike the bottom of the keyboard and bounce back. I stop typing and make myself present to any sound that reaches me. I become aware of a car starting not very far away. A bus goes by. I bring my presence back inside and immediately become aware of the taste of a banana I ate half an hour ago, then the feeling of my feet on the floor, then my pullover which is making me itch at a particular spot where it is touching my skin.

In the same way that we talk about a field of vision, we can talk about a field of presence and this can encompass my senses, what I can know of my body and any of the activities of my mind. When I am with a panorama, this is both the field of my vision and the field of my presence. I am putting my presence in my vision and putting my vision at the service of my presence. I can then adjust the scope of my presence and the scope of my vision either to see the whole landscape or to home in on some far distant detail.

> I am standing on a viewing platform at the Aiguille du Midi, near Mont Blanc, looking out over the whole chain of the Alps, marvelling at the view. My eye is drawn to a village, its church and then its steeple. Suddenly I become aware of a slight, very local, disturbance in my hair. Now I am completely present to this part of my head, aware that this is how it feels when an insect has landed on me.

## Awarenesses

Each time my presence moves, as soon as it settles, I become aware of something. Just as the image in a kaleidoscope takes a new, stable position, just as jelly 'takes' or 'gels' into a shape that can be apprehended, after my presence has shifted, what I then become aware of 'gels' into a new awareness.

My presence is drawn to each of the tiny events above and an awareness is produced. I have to *become* aware of each of these events before I can say I *am* aware of them. In each case, the result is an awareness. Then my presence shifts, it moves or adjusts. Each awareness takes place within the scope of my presence as it is there and then.

To say of something that "it came into my mind," is equivalent to saying that I was present to it and that this resulted in an awareness.

In the example, I stopped typing the text and instead of continuing with that train of thought, I let myself be present to the world around me. It so happened that my presence moved to my hearing. I started to listen, which is to say that I had in me a series of unspoken questions: What could I hear at this instant? and now? and now? and I was immediately aware of the answers. Each new sound drew my presence. This led to an awareness of what it was. This in turn caused me to adjust my presence to listen to the sound more appropriately. Awarenesses and adjustments continued while the car came and went, and then my presence was drawn by a new sound, the bus.

To go about one's life is to have an endless succession of awarenesses.

Notice that in talking about 'an awareness', Gattegno went beyond the conventional use of the word 'awareness' in English. He spoke French many years before he spoke English and needed an English equivalent to the French expression *une prise de conscience*, because the concept it describes was essential to his vision of humans and human education. (See Appendix A for a longer discussion of this.)

### Questions and 'aha' moments

I am familiar with climates within me in which my mind is preoccupied for some time by a question or a problem. It is easy to recognize that one has an unanswered question or a problem, since this creates an inner tension. For Gattegno, a problem *is* a tension. He suggests that this is why we call the answer to a problem a 'solution': the problem is solved when the tension has been dis-solved. Indeed, it is precisely because of the tension we feel that each of us is aware that he has a problem or a question. As long as the tension remains, the problem is un(dis)solved.

When the question and its answer are practically simultaneous, as in the earlier example, no perceptible tension is created.

If a question remains with me, the tension associated with it may grow. In this case, when I finally have an answer - in the form, of course, of an awareness - it releases this tension and is accompanied by an "Ah!". The intensity of the "Ah!" is proportional to the amount of tension created by, and associated with, the question.

So, I know how important a question is to me through the amount of tension it creates within me.

As an example, let us consider the awareness that Archimedes experienced, which led to him running through the streets shouting "Eureka!" with such excitement that the echo comes down to us two thousand two hundred years later.

> Archimedes had a problem. The King had asked him to determine whether or not the goldsmith who had created the new crown had actually used all the gold given to him to make it. To decide this, both its weight and volume had to be measured. It was easy to weigh the crown, but how would it be possible to measure the exact volume of an irregular object like a crown without melting it down to an ingot? This question had been with Archimedes for some time, creating a tension which, we can suppose, became stronger as the days went by. I imagine a tired, dispirited Archimedes, deciding to give up for the day and relax. I

see him stepping into his bath, gently sinking down into the hot water and noticing as he does so that the level of the water rises. Suddenly, the different elements come together and "gel" into an awareness - if he places the crown in a container filled to the brim with water and measures the volume of water which overflows, he will have measured the volume of the crown. "Eureka!"

But what interests us here, beyond Archimedes' solution, is that we can safely make some quite precise statements about what happened during his bath, if bath there was ...

It was certainly not his first bath; if it had been, he would have been too present to the sensations of the water on his body to have the freedom of mind necessary for this gelling of awareness to take place. The water was not too hot, nor too cold. If either had been the case, he would have been too taken by the discomfort to think of anything else. If the bath over-flowed, he was not worried about mopping up the water. Nothing about the bath was new to Archimedes. What was new was the coming together of the relevant facts in such a way as to permit a new awareness to take place.

Because I am human, like Archimedes, I can guess that he was probably not thinking about anything in particular, perhaps not even anything much at all. This is an inner climate in which many important awarenesses take place. Many people know this through personal experience and it has been documented by scientists and others talking about their discoveries.

## Scientific discoveries are awarenesses
All scientific discoveries without exception are awarenesses. At some time in history, someone has been examining a problem, turning it over in his mind until its elements have come together in such a way as to produce an "Ah!" or an "Of course!" or any of the other expressions which we use to say "I have become aware of ...". The history of science is the history of thinkers becoming aware of models which organise facts. The content of an awareness or a cascade of awarenesses creates a model which allows them to better understand the world in which we live.

As long as no one has become aware of a phenomenon as such, the concept which will model it remains unknown to everybody. So, the concept of acceleration was unknown to the ancient Greeks, although every little Greek boy and girl, like all children, had rolled down hills, run and fallen down while playing. But no Greek ever asked himself questions which would allow him to develop a concept of acceleration which we can recognise. For a phenomenon to become a field of scientific study, it is necessary for someone somewhere to become aware of it.

As one would expect, up to now almost all scientists and other thinkers in the West have attended to the content of their awareness - to the facts they have become aware of - rather than looking at the process of becoming aware. Imagine how unlikely it would have been for Archimedes to make his discovery and instead of shouting "Eureka!" to have said instead, "My goodness, I've just had an awareness. How did that happen?" This is why this field of study has taken so long to appear.

Caleb Gattegno proposes this field as the foundation of the science of education: the study of awareness, the process of becoming aware and the resulting awarenesses.

The many examples of people becoming aware of new ways of viewing reality can interest us for several reasons. As members of a civilisation, we can understand it better by looking at the people who have marked it. Those who made these discoveries have often spoken of how their ideas came to them, how their awarenesses gelled, which means that some of these awarenesses have been documented. They constitute a field of study of the phenomenon of awareness as such. Discoveries as different as that of the structure of benzene by August Kekule, half asleep in his kitchen, or of Isaac Singer becoming aware that in order to mechanise sewing it was necessary to put the hole in the other end of the needle, are good examples.

But the spectacular awarenesses which led to advances in the sciences should not dazzle us into overlooking the more important fact: that the whole lifetime of each and every human being is made up of awarenesses. It is by and through our awarenesses that we have learnt all we know and that we function in the world we live in, and this is true from the very beginning of our lives.

This being so, we now have the means to investigate all areas of human development using the light of awareness and awarenesses. In the field of education, we can exhaustively identify the awarenesses needed in any domain, and redefine teaching as the activity which leads students to cover this ground for themselves without missing any essential steps and without wasting time. Gattegno demonstrated this with thousands of students in hundreds of classrooms around the world.

# Further reading

*The Science of Education, Part 1 Theoretical Considerations*

# 2  The self

Gattegno proposed that it would be possible to recast the history and present functioning of the universe, including everything that happens on earth, in terms of the evolution and transformation of energy.

Clearly, the human body can be seen as energy. But to account for all human activities, for all the inner climates and states in which we live our lives (including emotions, sentiments and traits of character), for all our varied ways of thinking, being and behaving, and for our capacity for self-observation, Gattegno developed a model in which he distinguished three forms that human energy takes. He called these the self, the psyche and affectivity. He described their characteristics, how they relate to each other and how they function together.

For any human being, living a life demands that two very different requirements be met. The first is to be able to change and evolve. The second is to be able to maintain the status quo, which *inter alia* gives one the certainty of being the same person from day to day. In Gattegno's vision of human beings, the self is responsible for change, while the psyche is the name given to the element which maintains the status quo.

Affectivity is the name he gave to the energy found throughout the body which the self can 'affect' (or assign[1]) to all the tasks it undertakes. Like the self, affectivity is therefore turned towards the present and the immediate future.

In this chapter we will be looking at the self.

\* \* \*

How is it that in spite of all the changes which have taken place in me since the beginning of my life, I recognize myself as 'the same person'? I

---

[1] Gattegno first used 'affectivity' in French, where the meanings of the verb affecter include 'to assign' or 'to allot'.

am no longer the little girl I was at five, nor the adolescent I was at fifteen. Both my weight and my height are different. My skin has wrinkles, my face has changed. My tastes are not at all the same. I never play hopscotch as I did the year I turned eight. I no longer love the person I had a crush on when I was fourteen. I am no longer moved by what moved me at twenty. How is it that I have such a strong feeling of unity in spite of the fact that so many things about me have changed? Where does the certainty come from that I am the same person as I was in spite of all these changes I see in myself?

We all know that ever since we learnt to talk we have always spoken of ourselves as "I". If I ask someone, "Who thinks when you think?" he will answer, "I do!" "When you write, who writes?" "I do!" To examine this entity we need to give it a name. Gattegno called it "the self".

He described the self as an energy that is free and creative: free in that it may choose to engage with any unknown it meets and creative in that when doing so it may create a response. Since it is an energy, it is not an object. But it does have many attributes, including awareness, will, sensitivity, vulnerability, intelligence, patience and the sense of truth (the sense which tells us that what we are perceiving belongs to reality). The role of the self is to meet the unknown and to learn.

The self is that in me which knows; which knows it knows; which knows itself; which is open to meeting the inner and outer world, and either recognises what it meets or knows that what it meets is unknown. The self is adapted to meeting the unknown and, as we shall see, is equipped to do so.

It is the self which is aware of being the same self today as yesterday and the day before yesterday, but which also knows that it lives and evolves in time. The self is the part of me which becomes aware.

The self is not something mysterious. It is not something hidden or esoteric, although one can live one's life without noticing it in action. It can be encountered in two different ways. First, it can be considered as a concept which will allow us to notice and understand many phenomena which have been largely ignored. As such, it allowed Gattegno to build a more complete, more dynamic model of Man than those constructed up to now in the West. However it is also possible to become aware of the self experientially, to be in direct contact with the self as a form of energy; one can do this by sensitising oneself to its energetic reality.

Since the self is the learner in each of us, teachers need to encounter at least the attribute of the self that is awareness in this second, experiential fashion: to be brought into direct contact with their awareness as it functions from moment to moment. This sensitivity must be developed in any serious programme of teacher education. The Science of Education that Gattegno developed certainly requires this because the awareness is its basic unit.

The self is an energy. Compared to the other energies of which we are formed or which are within us, the self is minute. However, this does not hinder it from acting. An army of thousands of men is under the command of a single individual, and a chain is always established which allows orders to reach the soldier who is furthest from the seat of command. In the case of humans, the self is the seat of command. An expression Gattegno used very often was "the self is at the helm", by which he meant, at the helm of the 'ship' that is me crossing the ocean of my life.

The self is an energy. As an energy, it can recognize energy movements which take place both in and around its body, the system it has given itself. Internally, the self recognises the movements of energy associated, for example, with emotions and somatic dysfunctions. For detecting energy whose origin is external, each self builds itself a set of sensitive instruments, the sense organs. In modern times, we have learnt to extend our sense organs by constructing physical instruments which complement and are often more sensitive than those we naturally give ourselves.

## The attributes of the self

To determine what the attributes (i.e. the characteristics) of the self might be, Gattegno asked himself what qualities all humans possess that could not be acquired by a young child interacting with his environment. He examined the varied engagements of human lives, identifying in detail the movements of the mind involved and the characteristics of the mind that are required to produce them. He then asked himself: "Can this characteristic be learnt from the environment? Can it be acquired from outside?" If it could not, he considered it to be an attribute of the person, and more specifically to be an attribute of the self. Using this criterion, he made up a list of these attributes as below. (1986 XVI 2-4:11-13)

Note that Gattegno's way of studying a complex subject like the self was to highlight it from different angles, each new 'lighting' throwing some aspects of the subject into relief and others into shadow. When sufficient lightings have been cast, a sense of the subject emerges. He considered that this was the only satisfactory way of studying complex problems and called this way of knowing 'intuition'.

At any particular moment, many attributes of the self can usually be seen to be at work. To identify and describe them, though, we need to highlight them one at a time.

## Awareness

Awareness is the most basic of the attributes of the self. We cannot 'learn' awareness, nor teach it; and especially not to babies or to small children, who clearly display through their behaviour that they already function using their awareness. Only I can become aware for myself. Only I can direct my awareness to what I want to investigate when I engage myself in the activities I decide to take up, or extract myself from activities I decide to abandon. This is true whatever my age and whatever the activity.

Awareness is omnipresent in our inner lives. However, we can ask ourselves whether there was ever a period in anyone's life during which there was no awareness. If I look at the evolution of my own life, can I find a time when I wasn't aware? Obviously, on the day of my birth, I was not yet aware of what a lifetime of awarenesses has brought me. I had no idea that language existed or that political parties operated in the society in which I then lived. I could not have chosen my profession. In fact, I was not aware of almost all that now occupies my mind. This is the case because we live in time and exchange our time for experience. Individuals evolve over their lifetime.

The propositions that consciousness only appears at birth or with the advent of language were considered to be both untenable and useless by Gattegno. Although the word 'consciousness' appears in his early writings, he soon abandoned it in favour of 'awareness', which he did not equate with consciousness[2]. He pointed out that if one strokes the skin on the face of a new-born baby with a feather, one can see immediately that it is aware of this, that it feels the sensation of the feather on that part of its skin. If a loud noise is made beside it, the baby demonstrates that it is aware of it by moving its head. Any useful model of human development must explain this, and further, explain how a baby can grip a finger which touches its palm. For Gattegno, the baby must have learnt to use its hands before birth and therefore must have been aware *in utero*. This proposition was

---

[2] For more discussion of this, see Appendix A.

outlandish when he published it in the early 1970's, but is now widely accepted as a result of the findings of modern medical technology.

Many scientists believe that the mind emerges from the activity of the brain, and since the embryonic brain begins to develop about two weeks after the fertilisation of the egg, they conclude that the mind could date at the very earliest from this time. Gattegno had a different vision. To consider the mind as emerging from the brain did not allow him as coherent an understanding of a whole human over a whole lifetime as supposing that the mind creates the brain it requires. In *The Mind Teaches the Brain* (1975), Gattegno developed this idea in three Parts, arguing firstly that "In the Beginning There is the Self Not the Brain," where he concluded that the self must necessarily be present in the first cell; secondly that, "The Brain Alone Cannot Generate a Complex Human Life"; and thirdly that, "The Mind Always Educates the Brain," which extended his study into areas of human experience rarely considered in association with the brain, even today.

In Gattegno's model then, the self is present in the first cell, this cell being the union of an ovum, a spermatozoon and a self. Since the self is not an object but an energy, it occupies no space in this cell. And since awareness is an attribute of the self, it is as much a part of the first cell as the DNA. Awareness remains with us for as long as life lasts.

In this model, Gattegno proposes that as humans we do not live time as the continuum that is suggested by a phrase like 'the stream of consciousness'. Instead, we live a series of discrete moments, of discrete movements of the mind, each of which he called 'an awareness', because we are aware of the content.

> I am opening my neighbour's front door with her key. I know that keys can only go into locks one way so I make myself aware of the shape of the lock and then look at the key to become aware if it is correctly oriented in my fingers. I present the key to the lock and when I am aware that they are perfectly aligned I push the key right in and test if it is free to turn.

Within a second or two, I have had at least four or five significant awarenesses.

Working on awareness and awarenesses is the most important aspect of teaching as it is practised within the framework of Gattegno's Science of Education. It will be studied in detail, with practical examples, in Part II of this book starting at Chapter 5.

## Concentration

When I am awake, I am usually concentrated on one thing or another. The energy of my self is gathered so that I am present to some well-defined task. Put another way, when I am concentrated, I am focussed.

> I walk round my garden and am present to the general state of the beds. I become aware of a patch which needs weeding. To do this, I need to concentrate on each seedling, recognising it (if I can) as a weed or a flower to decide if it should be pulled out or not. I gauge with care the force I will exert to pull the seedling out without breaking the stem. Then my state of concentration dissolves, I move on to the next seedling and find myself concentrated again.

To read a book involves concentration in at least two very different ways. As I take in the first words I exclude from my field of awareness everything around me. I am now concentrated on what is to be read. This focussing, this polarisation of my being on what I am reading, is necessary if I want to lift any meaning from the page. I will remain concentrated in this way for as long as I remain engrossed in the book.

However, at the same time, I need to accomplish the act of reading, and this relies on a process of successive concentrations. My eyes focus on the first few words and when I have taken them in, this concentration dissolves and is renewed a few words further along. I keep the content of each period of concentration within me until I reach the end of the sentence and then the words dissolve and I retain only the meaning. Thus in reading, we can see a succession of micro-concentrations and micro-deconcentrations.

These two different ways of concentrating become obvious when I occasionally stop reading to think and become aware that my eyes have continued to 'read'.

When I was a child learning to read, my self was responsible for this process but I automatised it when I was six or seven years old and when I read now I can use my time to construct the mental images the words evoke and to respond to them. My self no longer has to create the succession of micro-concentrations, they appear to just happen.

Concentration is the usual state of the self during the waking hours. (What we do when we sleep will be dealt with in Chapter 3.) This is the case from the beginning of life, and continues throughout, whether I am concentrated on how and where to place my centre of gravity and which muscles to flex in order to stand up around the age of one, on the positioning of the latest addition to my stamp collection as a teenager, or on writing a book now.

In a state of concentration, I can fix for myself a set of sensory thresholds below which I will not allow myself to be disturbed. These thresholds can vary considerably and there can be several for the same sense at any one time. Thus a mother who is reading can set thresholds such that she is not disturbed by a loud noise coming from outside - a clap of thunder, for example - but will hear a much softer noise made by her sleeping baby in the next room.

Sometimes, while concentrated on something, I feel a call coming from somewhere on my skin which tells me that this place requires scratching. I can respond to this call without feeling disturbed because the de-concentration that the interruption demands is so minute compared to what is holding me in the main activity.

Concentration does not require energy. It is spontaneous and natural. It is not difficult to concentrate. In fact, it is quite difficult to be anything other than concentrated, since the simple fact of undertaking an activity - any activity - leads to a state of concentration.

It is sometimes said of children that they cannot concentrate for more than a few minutes at a time. Some psychologists have even given fairly precise figures in this area. One has only to look at children playing to know that this is not true. What is true is that if we ask children to concentrate on something which does not interest them at all and forbid them any alternative physical activity, then they do exactly what adults do - they take refuge in their inner lives and wait to be freed. This situation can be observed in many schools throughout the world. It is created by adults and does not reflect on the capacity of children to concentrate for extended periods.

Once I know that concentration is the normal state of the self, my students' state of concentration in the classroom informs me about their degree of involvement. It informs me as to whether the challenge I have proposed to them is well matched to their current capacity, neither too easy nor too hard. If the challenge is not adapted, I know I must intervene immediately in order to give them one likely to involve them more completely. If I become aware that the students are focusing on something other than the lesson, I have to stop and change.

If I mobilize my students at the level of their selves by giving them challenges they can become involved in, they will not be anything other than concentrated. Not only are they in a state of concentration, but they are concentrating on the subject matter in question.

## Presence and concentration

Let us return to the example of reading, an activity which readily allows us to study the movements of our presence and our varying degrees of concentration.

> I am sitting comfortably in an armchair reading a good novel. I am fully concentrated in the story when I become aware of my cat. It impinges upon my awareness several times, but each time I maintain my concentration and refuse to be present to it. Now the cat rubs its nose against my slipper, trying harder to interrupt my state of concentration and to draw my presence to it. I try to chase it away with vague movements of my arm, but then, to minimise the interruption, I invite it to jump into my lap and settle down. My mental images remain with the book. But finally, when my cat insists, I stop reading for long enough to really deal with it. I get up and feed it. Then I come back to the armchair and settle back down into my book again. It takes me a moment to lose my feeling of irritation at the interruption before I am completely immersed in the story again.

In this situation, it is possible to see the steady increase in my presence to the cat to the detriment of my concentration on the book, up to the moment when the cat's needs have been dealt with successfully.

The study of an activity such as reading is full of information for anyone wishing to understand the relationship between awareness, presence and concentration. It reveals the fact that the usual state of my waking life is one of concentration. Obviously other states exist; I can daydream, a state in which I recognize myself to be not present to anything in particular. This is a state I find myself in occasionally. But, like most people, I spend most of each day in a state of concentration.

When I have time before me, I make myself present to my absence of commitment and my self presents me with an activity. Once I am in it, I concentrate on it.

## The need to know

The need to know is an attribute of the self. This attribute is not limited to scientists or the privileged few. The need to know inhabits us all, and is visible in the small day to day activities of all human beings. For example, in the curiosity we experience and then express with phrases like: "I wonder who..." or "I'd love to know... ", and in children who break open a toy in order to find out how it works. For Gattegno, this state has an affective component as well as an intellectual one. The affective component is an energy which allows us to remain in contact with the problem once it has been noticed, until either our curiosity has been satisfied or we decide to let the problem go. The intellectual component concerns the object of our curiosity.

On a prosaic level, we find the need to know in an activity as ordinary as crossing a road. Examining this process, we can start by putting ourselves in contact with the judgments we make in order to cross at a suitable moment: the likely arrival time of oncoming cars, the distance I can cover in a given time, etc. After that, we can become aware of the subtle movements of the self which demanded that these judgments be made, and which were manifestations of the need to know.

A need to know like this may seem trivial, but the advantage of recognising the need to know in such occurrences is that we then have dozens of opportunities to study it every day. These moments illustrate the fact that this attribute need not be expressed verbally; young adults rarely have an explicit inner dialogue about crossing a road, for example. (But the need for an inner dialogue in this situation does increase with age!) And during the embryonic period of life and in early childhood the need to know is lived intensely, but cannot be expressed verbally.

Once a child has learnt to speak, the need to know may of course manifest itself verbally but usually it does not. For example, when I learnt to skip as a little girl, a sensitive observer would have seen the need to know clearly manifested in the way I was mobilized into a dialogue with the physical world: working out the speed of the impulse to be given to the rope so that it was where it was supposed to be when I lifted myself off the ground, the rotation of my wrists so that the rope went under my feet correctly, the energies I had to mobilize to jump over the rope, the muscle tone and the coordination of my muscles to jump while I was turning. There were many things I needed to know to be able to skip.

When awareness itself is the object of enquiry, Gattegno pointed out that, "the need to know ... becomes awareness of awareness". (1983 XIII 2:12) And for those who wish to study education as it is presented here, the need to study 'awareness of awareness' leads us to the need for awareness ... of the awareness of awareness.

## Discrimination

Discrimination is the attribute of the self which allows it to detect difference where previously it perceived similarity.

> During a visit to a tapestry factory near Aubusson, I discovered that professional dyers could distinguish between twenty blues numbered from 561 to 580, where I could only just detect a difference between the first and the last.

Clearly the ability to discriminate between colours can be trained; it is the attribute of the self called discrimination that allows us to train ourselves to see colour better. The self education that leads up to the statement that "I can discriminate between x and y" is what Gattegno is drawing our attention to. He considered that the self's ability to educate itself in this way is something that must be there from the beginning, for when did it appear if not then?

Perfume designers, wine tasters and chefs are among those who invest unusual amounts of time in developing their powers of discrimination, and their prowess sometimes amazes those who have never made similar investments.

In the classroom, I can count on the fact that this attribute of the self functions. This does not mean that my students can already discriminate appropriately within the domain of study, any more than the fact that perception is an attribute means that no learning is necessary in order to perceive the outside world. It does mean, though, that if I present a language appropriately, my students' power of discrimination will be mobilised, and they will educate themselves in the language. In fact, I can present it in such a way that their discrimination itself will also be educated, so that when they leave my class they will be more aware of their powers of discrimination than before and better able to use them. All this is simply because the students are human.

In language learning, discrimination is required to hear a distinction between what may at first appear to be similar sounds. It is what allows us to come to perceive the inner climate which reveals the need for this or that verb tense. It also draws out the distinction made by native speakers between two of their words where only one word exists for the same notions in the learner's language. (For example, where French has *savoir* and *connaître* for English 'know'.)

One of the jobs of the teacher is to create situations where students can explore the more subtle aspects of the language. Their power of discrimination will then be used extensively and often, giving them the opportunity to master what they are learning. They must be able to hear distinctions in phrases like "My hand's cold" and "My hands are cold", said with the reduced "are" that is typical of English. The difference between *nikko* and *niko* in spoken Japanese requires that the teacher invoke the students' capacity to discriminate, as does the difference in pronunciation between "Elle a vu" and "Elle l'a vu", spoken in French. And so does the understanding of the difference in meaning between "Il me l'a donné parce que je le lui ai demandé" and "Il me l'a donné parce que je la lui ai demandée".

## Perception

Perception is an attribute of the self. All of us are equipped for perceiving the world outside, with what people call "the five senses". But we should also consider inner perceptions: my capacity to be aware of the state of my body and the state of my mind. I perceive emotions, feelings and sentiments; moods, tastes and mental images ... and much, much more. Thus perception is concerned not only with what my senses bring to me, but also with my awareness of myself.

More generally, this attribute allows the self to become aware of changes of energy which take place within us. Obviously our sense organs have evolved so that I can be sensitive to the energy changes within them that are provoked by events outside. But to be hungry, I must also have some kind of perception of a change in my energy stocks, and to recognise myself as being angry or fearful, I must perceive the particular coagulations and movements of energy that I learnt as a child to name as anger or fear.

The fact that perception is an attribute of the self means that perception can be educated, since my self is the learner in me. In fact, to reach a basic, functional education of listening, looking, taste, touch and smell takes several years of childhood. Gattegno described some of this learning in detail in The Universe of Babies. Both the attribute and the skill of perception then continue to be educated throughout one's life in all sorts of areas: driving cars, tasting food, endurance training, recognising the sound and feel of a perfectly hit ball, or things which are more obviously linked to perception like painting. But the capacity to perceive as such does not have to be learnt; it is there from the beginning.

When a language teacher has become aware that her students really do possess the attributes of perception and discrimination – awareness here being opposed to knowledge gained through reading, etc[3] - her way of working in the classroom will be transformed. She knows that her students can perceive both the world and the words used to describe it, and also that they can learn to discriminate between situations and phrases that may each initially appear to be similar. So rather than exaggerating differences to enable the students to perceive them easily, she can work in such a way as to train her students to perceive finer and finer differences. Then, as Gattegno proposed, the teacher is working on the students, while the students work on the language.

It is also important in language teaching to deal with the students' perception of their inner movements of energy – their sentiments, emotions, unease, knowledge, tastes ... To speak a language properly and comfortably requires the authentic expression of these inner states and climates, which is only possible if the students connect them directly with the appropriate words and conventions of the language being learnt. For such a direct connection to be made, the inner movements must exist and be perceived at the time the student speaks in the classroom. The process of association must be lived, not intellectualised via translation or the learning of rules.

## Will

The will is an attribute of the self. Will is not only the 'willpower' which allows a smoker to stop smoking, or the insistence of a 'wilful' person. The will that Gattegno is speaking about can be much subtler. In his model, he speaks of 'will' as that part of the self which is involved in modifying energy inside one's system. I place my hand on a flat surface - my will mobilises the energy for me to do so - and I lift my index finger just one millimetre. It is my will which acts on the energies of my hand and my arm in order to do this. It is not possible to do anything at all without the involvement of the will. "Our will is the response of the self whenever an energy transaction is considered." (1986 XVI 2-4:12) This definition differs somewhat from the one in everyday usage. However, the more usual definition of will as 'will power' is a natural extension of it.

---

[3] This distinction will be dealt with in chapter 7, but, briefly, the difference is that awarenesses transform a person so that he cannot but live their consequences, while knowledge is stored and retrieved but does not transform.

Teachers sometimes complain that students lack the will to learn. But this can only be their students' response to the particular demands being made on them by the teacher, not a general lack, since both the will and learning permeate every aspect of their lives. The will is present in all we do, in the classroom and throughout our lives.

Knowing this, I know that in my teaching I can rely on the existence of an ever responsive will in my students. But to recognize the students' will in action, I first have to know my own. Gattegno, writing of the role of the teacher, stated:

> There are four tasks facing a teacher who wants to subordinate teaching to learning. The first is to become a person who knows himself and others as persons. This is no mere sentimental homily, but means that a teacher must recognize that beyond any individual's behaviour is a will which changes behaviours and integrates them. ... Of all the powers of the mind, it is our will that permits us to become persons. (1971:84)

However, I know, too, that if my students are having problems learning what I am trying to teach, I will only make matters worse by simply demanding feats of memorisation from them, the effort for which has to be sustained by their will alone. To do this is to ask the students to spend excessive and unreasonable amounts of energy and time to overcome my lack of teaching skills. Instead, my teaching should address itself to other attributes of the self: the students' capacity to image, to imagine, to act, to perceive, and so on.

To ask students to memorise when other attributes of the self can be used is not a legitimate use of the will. Using one's will to drive memorisation does not yield learning that will stand the test of time. We all know this because all of us have lived, or watched others live, hundreds of hours in mathematics, history or foreign language classrooms where memorisation yielded very meagre results.

The will is called into play when any movement, any behaviour is required. This means that it is also needed when changes in a behaviour are going to be put in place. For example, the possibility of giving oneself a good accent in a foreign language depends upon the relationship one has built between one's self and one's psyche. Introducing a new behaviour such as learning to say a French "r" or an English "th" requires the students to mobilise their will. In this domain, each student must will himself to intervene in the normal functioning of his psyche so as to control the voluntary muscles he uses to speak, the functioning of which he made automatic years before while learning his mother tongue.

The student cannot concentrate on all aspects of his production in the foreign language at the same time. But the teacher can encourage him to go back over what he is saying several times, integrating some new variable on each occasion - the word order, the pronunciation, the melody of the sentence, the rhythm, the intonation - until it sounds as if he has captured at least something of the spirit of the language. Knowing the dynamics of the interplay between the psyche and the self, she can propose to the student that she become his discipline on a temporary basis, i.e. that she can will him to repeatedly re-enter his psyche and make the changes needed for all aspects of the utterance to be correct.

## Action

Action is an attribute of the self. Action, "combines perception and the will to assess the correct amounts of energy needed to perform the activities the self gets engaged in." (1986 XVI 2-4:12) Action as an attribute is not, therefore, the body movement itself, but that which makes it possible for the self to initiate, examine and refine this movement. With this understanding, we can see how it is possible to learn physical activities. From the start of our lives, this attribute of the self enables us to develop two complementary sets of abilities: the ability to choose how to act given a purpose we have in mind, and the ability to predict what the consequences of a given act will be (both the effect on the outside world and how it feels to perform the act). We use feedback from our acts and their results to improve these abilities[4]. Generally, they are then automatised.

Learning physical activities provides repeated examples of these feedback mechanisms, as will be seen in Part 2 of this book. Learning with and from another person also involves feedback mechanisms, but now the action of each participant is a source of feedback for both.

## Intelligence

Intelligence is an attribute of the self. It is intelligence which allows the self to look for new ways of doing things or new answers to old questions, usually when existing solutions for whatever reason no longer seem satisfactory. That said, in the minds of people who are regarded as "intelli-

---

[4] These abilities rely on what in neuroscience are called the inverse and forward internal models respectively (Wolpert et al., 2001).

gent", the spontaneous generation of alternatives may become a matter of course.

We engage in an activity. Here is how Gattegno describes what is happening.

> The past is present in the use of all that is in the soma, the brain, the mind; the present activity is sustained by concentration, by selection of what to use, and by using it; the future is represented by intelligence that surveys the manner in which the present uses the past and, if need be, brings more of the past to bear in the situation or affects the concentration in the activity and the selection of what to use in it. (1988a:172)

In other words, the role of intelligence is to watch over situations being lived, to assess what the psyche is doing, and to generate new initiatives and act on them if this appears to be necessary or useful.

Gattegno speaks of,

> ... intelligent eating and intelligent control of the digestive tube so that the self disciplines itself to produce socially acceptable forms of feeding and evacuating ... intelligent breathing to avoid being out of breath in situations not calling for it ... intelligent seeing, hearing, feeling, and so on. (1988a:174)

Further, he says that, "if there is a somatic intelligence, there is also an intelligence of actions, an intelligence of feelings, of thoughts, of relationships, of organisation, of decision making, of compromise, ..." (1988a:180). For Gattegno, the conventional use of the word intelligence is damagingly limited. Irrespective of any academic achievements, Pelé was an intelligent footballer. To be an intelligent footballer is to be able to generate options and act on them.

Intelligence allows us to transform situations. It suggests to a student a new way of looking at a problem in maths, for example, or a tentative generalisation in language learning. But intelligence relies on understanding in order to operate. No one can transform a situation which is not understood. To ensure that the situation is indeed understood, a good way is usually for the students themselves to have constructed it, guided if necessary by astute questioning from the teacher designed to ensure that the awarenesses that are required do take place.

In classes of maths, of grammar, or of language, intelligence is seen to be at work when students show a desire to generate a number of different points of view for a given situation.

Since intelligence is an attribute of the self, it can be educated. Trial, error and engagement with the consequences of a trial, all 'sharpen the blade' that is intelligence, giving students the experience of how to function intelligently. Rote learning and repetition dull the blade.

### Sensitivity and vulnerability
Sensitivity and vulnerability function together as attributes of the self.

Sensitivity is the attribute that puts the self in contact with what the senses produce. Starting from the relatively undifferentiated input perceived by a new-born baby, the self educates itself to be sensitive to more and more detail, until it determines that its senses are functioning adequately for the tasks it must perform. This will vary from person to person. The dyers of Aubusson (mentioned above) have used their sensitivity to continue the education of their colour vision beyond the point where most people would abandon it in the absence of any worthwhile return. Writers develop sensitivities to the register, connotations and impact of words, to the rhythm and balance of sentences, and so on. As such sensitivities are developed, they become increasingly coordinated as the self knits them together.

Vulnerability in Gattegno's vision is not used in the conventional way, where a vulnerable person is one who might easily be hurt. In this case, the vulnerability describes a weakness of the psyche or soma.

For Gattegno, vulnerability is the attribute of the self which allows it to regulate the impact that the outside world can have on us through our senses. Thus it is necessary, ubiquitous and beneficial, since it allows the self either to open itself, to broaden its way of perceiving the world, or to protect itself if necessary. To perceive more and more of the world I must open my senses to it, allow myself to be vulnerable to what it can offer and increase my sensitivity to whatever crosses the threshold. However, in some situations, for example after a natural disaster, it may be necessary for practical reasons to reduce my vulnerability, in this case perhaps my vulnerability to the suffering around me.

In the classroom, the teaching of all subjects implies work on sensitivity and vulnerability. Gattegno sees a teacher presenting situations which have the potential to educate the sensitivity of the students, and at the same time which invite and inspire them to make themselves vulnerable to what their sensitivity can detect.

One aspect of learning to express oneself effectively with language, whether native or foreign, is for learners to become more and more aware of the impact of words on listeners and readers, a sensitivity that good speakers and writers have developed. Writing a poem out of 30 words chosen randomly is an exercise that develops this, because the students have to make themselves vulnerable to the gamut of meanings each word can express, sensitive to the parts of speech each can occupy, and sensitive, too, to the effect that any one word has on its neighbours.

It should be said that working on vulnerability in this way has nothing to do with using stratagems whose only role is to make students feel secure and socially at ease in the classroom. In fact, if each student has his self at the helm, then social fears that arise in the psyche disappear.

## Abstraction

Abstraction is an attribute of the self, with more than one form. In addition to the power to formulate a general concept from the qualities of specific examples, Gattegno described abstraction using the term "stressing and ignoring". This is the process by which we highlight certain awarenesses in some field while others recede into the background.

At first glance the effect may resemble concentration. But concentration allows us to limit our attention to the field we are working on, while abstraction allows us to choose what we attend to within the field. A city map offers us an opportunity to watch the two at work. If I am looking for a hospital, I consult the key for the appropriate symbol and then set myself to see only that symbol as I scan the map, stressing it and ignoring the others. Within moments, the other features fade into the background. While I am doing this, it is my concentration on the map and the task which excludes the rest of the environment - the noise of my computer, for example - from my awareness.

The writing of a book also illustrates the difference. Writing requires concentration inasmuch as one must be focussed on the task. However, writing this chapter, for example, required that we highlight in ourselves the various attribute of the self that were being examined, with the awarenesses that this highlighting generated, while other attributes of the self which in life are there to be called upon at all times – and which were certainly there during the writing - were deliberately ignored.

The use of abstraction is not limited to adults. The baby who does not panic despite the many changes visible in his mother — with or without makeup, dressed in blue yesterday and in red today, hair done this way one day and that way another, wet or dry — shows a sophisticated capacity for abstraction. He has clearly learnt to stress what is constant in her, and ignore much of what changes. Even a summary investigation of babies shows that they live in a world in which abstraction is constantly necessary and always available.

Learning to talk is another good example where abstraction must be used by infants. An infant must extract from the noises he hears those which belong to human speech; extract from the speech of the environment qualities such as intonation, stress and melody, and voice qualities like tenderness or anger; not allow himself to be distracted by elements which do not yet have meaning for him - the vocabulary and the syntax, for example. To do all this, an infant requires a highly developed capacity for abstraction. Yet this is done by infants in the months before their first birthday.

To be able to use the word "chair" for everything which has four legs, a seat and a back, whatever the colour or the shape, a child must know how to make abstractions.

As another demonstration that small children use abstraction in the sense of creating new concepts from the qualities of specific examples, Gattegno pointed to the appearance in their speech of pronouns and, more particularly, of the word "I". A pronoun is a class of classes. To use the word "chair" for a class of impressions is an abstraction at a first level. To then use "it" to speak of the chair, it is necessary to abstract from all the classes that are individual nouns to create a second level of abstraction. But to manage to use "I", the meaning of which is never made visible by the eye-movements or gestures of other speakers, children must use mental dynamics. The meaning of this pronoun is difficult to capture. For all the other pronouns, there is a physical movement associated with the word. When people say "you", they turn towards the person they are talking to. When they use "him", they turn towards the listener or someone else, but never towards the person referred to as "him". But when they use "I", they never turn towards anyone. They can be looking at the listener, at someone else, or at no one in particular. To extract "I" from the environment, therefore, it is necessary to create a class of a class for a word which has no visible reference, an example of multi-level abstraction. It is easy to see why "I" is almost always the last of the pronouns to appear in the language of children in any culture.

## Freedom

Freedom is an attribute of the self. At its most conspicuous it is seen in the desire for political freedom for which men go to war, but the wellspring of this desire is made up of all the 'little freedoms' we have experienced from the start of our lives. A new-born baby is free to decide when he will empty his bladder, when he will wake up and when he will go to sleep. He is the one who knows if he is feeling uncomfortable and decides that his discomfort merits crying. He decides that his activity for the next few minutes will be to suck his thumb rather than his big toe. These examples teach us that the new-born baby knows a state of great freedom.

It is not surprising, then, that people know how to recognize political freedom later in their lives, and that they end up resisting those who attempt to take it from them. They know freedom because it is intimately known to us all, and want it everywhere in their lives because it is an attribute of the self.

At the level of the direction that I give to my self for the next few minutes, no one else can intervene. My inner life is free.

In the classroom, it is the students who put themselves into whatever activity is proposed and they are the ones who take themselves out of it, whatever their age and whatever the activity. Knowing this, the teacher can use her students' expressions of freedom to judge whether her teaching is adequate or not.

There is another level of freedom we can entertain. Gattegno proposed many times that one of the roles of the teacher is to free her students, by making them independent, autonomous and responsible. She does not do this all at once, but moment by moment and step by step.

The question of freeing our students will be dealt with in the discussion of the subordination of teaching to learning in Volume 2.

## Imaging and imagination

Imaging is the attribute of the self which, according to Gattegno, allows it to use the sense organs in reverse as tools for evocation. Imaging therefore contrasts with perception. Perception informs the self of the nature of energies coming in from outside, whereas imaging uses the sensory systems to restructure energies that originate in the brain. This creates evocations, which are a powerful tool for learning, as some of the experiences described in the second part of this volume will show.

In seeing and hearing, the energy of photons or sound waves is added into the system, so the images created come 'free of cost'. The parts of these images that we later have access to can be evoked, also at no appreciable cost. Although sight and hearing are most commonly associated with mental imagery, touch, taste and smell can also be evoked, sometimes years later and with astonishing freshness.

Consciously constructed mental images, on the other hand, require the spending of energy in order to be formed, but the results are usually easy to evoke with precision and often long lasting. In mathematics teaching, for example, it is possible to get students to construct mental images for almost all situations and thus to remove the need to memorise formulae, theorems etc. In language teaching, holding up a number of fingers which correspond to the number of words in a sentence, so that students can 'read' the sentence off, shows mental imagery at work, since each student has to mentally place the words on the fingers. This helps to establish word order and to improve fluency.

Imagination differs from imaging in that the results are not simply reproductions of pre-existing images, but are developed by the self which restructures the images in any way it wants. The self knows that it is making these changes. To evoke the Eiffel Tower in one's mind's eye is to image. To see it bend at the knees and take a drink from the Seine is to imagine.

Imaging is fundamental to animal and human existence, and imaging and imagination are of fundamental importance in education.

### The sense of truth
The sense of truth watches over all that the senses bring to us. It allows the self to know whether the reality that one constructs out of what one perceives is coherent and consistent with the rest of our reality, and can therefore be trusted.

From a different perspective, the sense of truth is,

> ... the attribute of the self which allows it to actually reach the reality of time and energy in every involvement and to 'recognize' i.e. be aware, that it is one's time and one's energy which are being involved in the activity under consideration. (1986 XVI 2-4:12)

In other words, the sense of truth operates in conjunction with awareness all the time so that, for each awareness, we can judge whether we are in a reality we know, in which we are firmly grounded. "To give up reliance on one's sense of truth is the greatest traumatism for anyone, for its guidance is needed at every moment and at all ages." (1988b:107)

What place is there for the sense of truth in the classroom? During a visit to a first grade class in California, Gattegno was scandalized when after the teacher had asked the children: "2 + 3?", they answered: "5?" as a question. This incident so marked Gattegno that he was still speaking of it thirty-five years later. What can be heard in the way they answered, is that they have learnt to abandon reliance on their own sense of truth and have moved into a system in which only the teacher has criteria to know if the answer is correct. These children were perfectly capable of knowing that 2 + 3 = 5, and certainly did know it, but they had understood that only the teacher had the right to know that he knew. This state of affairs is normal if teaching is considered to be the transmission of knowledge; in this case, the inevitable starting point is that only the teacher really knows. In these conditions, teaching is not based on the sense of truth of the students.

This example shows how a dysfunction can become installed without the teacher being aware of what she is doing, in this case undermining from the very beginning the foundations of the mathematics these children will study in years to come.

For a second example, we can turn to the teaching diary that John Holt published as "How Children Fail". The entry is worth quoting at length.

> October 1, 1959
>
> Not long ago Dr. Gattegno taught a demonstration class at Lesley-Ellis School. I don't believe I will ever forget it. It was one of the most extraordinary and moving spectacles I have seen in all my life.
>
> The subjects chosen for this particular demonstration were a group of severely retarded children. There were about five or six fourteen- or fifteen-year-olds. Some of them, except for unusually expression-less faces, looked quite normal; the one who caught my eye was a boy at the end of the table. He was tall, pale, with black hair. I have rarely seen on a human face such anxiety and tension as showed on his. He kept darting looks around the room like a bird, as if enemies might come from any quarter left unguarded for more than a second. His tongue worked continuously in his mouth, bulging out first one cheek

and then the other. Under the table, he scratched—or rather clawed—at his leg with one hand. He was a terrifying and pitiful sight to see.

With no formalities or preliminaries, no icebreaking or jollying up, Gattegno went to work. It will help you see more vividly what was going on if, providing you have rods at hand, you actually do the operations I will describe. First he took two blue (9) rods, and between them put a dark green (6), so that between the two blue rods and above the dark green there was an empty space 3 cm long. He said to the group, "Make one like this." They did. Then he said, "Now find the rod that will just fill up that space." I don't know how the other children worked on the problem; I was watching the dark-haired boy. His movements were spasmodic, feverish. When he had picked a rod out of the pile in the center of the table, he could hardly stuff it in between his blue rods. After several trials, he and the others found that a light green (3) rod would fill the space.

Then Gattegno, holding his blue rods at the upper end, shook them, so that after a bit the dark green rod fell out. Then he turned the rods over, so that now there was a 6 cm space where the dark green rod had formerly been. He asked the class to do the same. They did. Then he asked them to find the rod that would fill that space. Did they pick out of the pile the dark green rod that had just come out of that space? Not one did. Instead, more trial and error. Eventually, they all found that the dark green rod was needed.

Then Gattegno shook his rods so that the light green fell out, leaving the original empty 3 cm space, and turned them again so that the empty space was uppermost. Again he asked the children to fill the space, and again, by trial and error, they found the needed light green rod. As before, it took the dark-haired boy several trials to find the right rod. These trials seemed to be completely haphazard.

Hard as it may be to believe, Gattegno went through this cycle at least four or five times before anyone was able to pick the needed rod without hesitation and without trial and error. As I watched, I thought, "What must it be like to have so little idea of the way the world works, so little feeling for the regularity, the orderliness, the sensibleness of things?" It takes a great effort of the imagination to push oneself back, back, back to the place where we knew as little as these children. It is not just a matter of not knowing this fact or that fact; it is a matter of living in a universe like the one lived in by very young children, a universe which is utterly whimsical and unpredictable, where nothing has anything to do with anything else—with this difference, that these children had come to feel, as most very young children do not, that this universe is an enemy.

Then, as I watched, the dark-haired boy *saw*! Something went "click" inside his head, and for the first time, his hand visibly shaking with excitement, he reached without trial and error for the right rod.

He could hardly stuff it into the empty space. It worked! The tongue going round in the mouth, and the hand clawing away at the leg under the table doubled their pace. When the time came to turn the rods over and fill the other empty space, he was almost too excited to pick up the rod he wanted; but he got it in. "It fits! It fits!" he said, and held up the rods for all of us to see. Many of us were moved to tears, by his excitement and joy, and by our realization of the great leap of the mind he had just taken.

After a while, Gattegno did the same problem, this time using a crimson (4) and yellow (5) rod between the blue rods. This time the black-haired boy needed only one cycle to convince himself that these were the rods he needed. This time he was calmer, surer; he knew.

Again using the rods, Gattegno showed them what we mean when we say that one thing is half of another. He used the white (1) and red (2), and the red and the crimson (4) to demonstrate the meaning of "half." Then he asked them to find half of some of the other rods, which the dark-haired boy was able to do. Just before the end of the demonstration Gattegno showed them a brown (8) rod and asked them to find half of half of it, and this too the dark-haired boy was able to do.

I could not but feel then, as I do now, that whatever his IQ may be considered to have been, and however he may have reacted to life as he usually experienced it, this boy, during that class, had played the part of a person of high intelligence and had done intellectual work of very high quality. When we think of where he started, and where he finished, of the immense amount of mathematical territory that he covered in forty minutes or less, it is hard not to feel that there is an extraordinary capacity locked up inside that boy.

It is the tragedy of his life that he will probably never again find himself with a man like Gattegno, who knows, as few teachers do, that it is his business to put himself into contact with the intelligence of his students, wherever and whatever that may be, and who has enough intuition and imagination to do it. He has not done much work with retarded children. but he saw in a moment what I might have taken days or weeks to find out, or might never have found out: that to get in touch with the intelligence of these children, to give them solid ground to stand and move on, he had to go way, way back, to the very beginning of learning and understanding. Nor was this all he brought to the session. Equally important was a kind of respect for these children, a conviction that under the right circumstances they could and would do first-class thinking. There was no condescension or pity in his manner, nor even any noticeable sympathy. For the duration of the class he and these children were no less than colleagues, trying to work out a tough problem - and working it out.

John Holt goes on in his comments to draw attention to the intelligence of the children[5], but we also clearly see that Gattegno first took them back to where he was absolutely sure he had found a solid foundation on which he could construct the lesson. At this point they could start to operate with their sense of truth.

From these examples, it is obvious why any teacher must become aware of the sense of truth in her students, so that she can do two things. First, to keep constantly in mind the need for the students to work in such a way that they rely on their own sense of truth, because this is how a secure foundation for their learning will be created. Second, to be alert to the possibility that previous teachers may not have based their teaching on the sense of truth, and thereby left the students with vague, disconnected notions that can at best be recited but are not understood. In this case a good teacher will go back and first ground all that has been done in the stu-

---

[5] Holt continues, "The point of this incident may be misunderstood; indeed, is being misunderstood. Many people, reading of Gattegno's work with these boys, will think I am saying that if Gattegno could have just spent enough time with them, he could have made them smart. That is not my point at all. What I am saying is that they were already smart. What Gattegno did, for an hour or so, was to put within their reach a miniature universe on which they could exercise the intelligence they already had, a universe in which they could do real things and see for themselves whether what they had done worked or not.
Many people, having finally realized that human intelligence in any broad and important sense is not fixed but highly variable, may be and indeed are drawing the wrong conclusion that we can now set out to "teach" intelligence just as we used to try to "teach" math or English or history. But it is just as true of intelligence as it has always been true of school subjects that teaching—"I know something you should know and I'm going to make you learn it"—is above all else what prevents learning.
We don't have to make human beings smart. They are born smart. All we have to do is stop doing the things that made them stupid." (1984:161)

dents' sense of truth and then introduce all that should have been done since, working in the same way. Thus she will connect them with the reality of the topic being studied.

## The sense of harmony or well-being

The sense of harmony, or well-being, is the attribute of the self which allows it to know that everything is in order throughout one's whole being. Its job is to monitor the psycho-somatic system, notice dysfunctionings and then make the self aware that something must be done. When the system is functioning correctly, the sense of well-being allows the self to know, "that it is free to engage in meeting what comes, the unknown, the future." (1986 XVI 2-4:13)

In Gattegno's model, the sense of well-being depends on a harmonious functioning of the self with respect to the psyche in the soma. It is not, however, synonymous with 'feeling good'. The sense of well-being can be active in a climber at 3,500 metres up a mountain when the temperature is minus ten and he is cold.

It is the sense of harmony which is disturbed when an apology we owe is overdue. The little niggle which keeps coming back tells us that something in our life is not in order.

The sense of well-being is active in an adolescent who makes himself unhappy in order to study the effects on himself of the unhappiness he gives himself. In this case, the self is at the helm, a learning experience is being lived fully and the sense of well-being does not signal a dysfunction.

## Surrender

Surrender is the attribute of the self which, when the self has confidence in its ability to handle whatever outside reality might produce, allows it to lay itself open to this reality without fear. "Surrender is the self's form of trust, independently of what there is to trust in the non-self." (1986 XVI 2-4:13)

Gattegno (1983 XIII 4:4) described good listening as involving surrender. One must find a space in oneself for what a speaker says, surrendering to his message before one can properly respond.

## Patience and wisdom

Patience is the attribute which, "consists in knowing that processes take their time and that to be 'with' one of them means to give the time it takes to perform what its inner demands require." (1986 XVI 2-4:13)

In our investigation of the world, when we, "let ourselves be educated by the problem", we surrender to it so that we allow the problem to take all the space it needs to develop in us, and we remain patient so that we give it the time it requires to do this. In this way we meet the problem as it is and not as we might want it to be. We do not commit prematurely to a partial solution, but instead remain at peace with the problem as yet unresolved.

From another viewpoint, the patient self knows that the will allows us to control ourselves, while that which is outside us is, by its very nature, essentially non-controllable. Once teachers know patience as a reality of life for themselves, they can help students to accept that much of what is outside remains beyond their control, while being very demanding in the domain of their inner life, using their will.

> Wisdom is the attribute of the self which is co-extensive with the self's ability to know all the time what is possible, and keeps itself within those bounds. (1986 XVI 2-4:13)

## Objectivation
Objectivation is the word given by Gattegno to the attribute of the self which produces objects. It allows us to mobilize energies in the environment in order to change them into either somatic structures, psychic structures or physical structures.

Throughout life, the self mobilizes energies which are present in the environment in order to create the man-made world we have around us. The creation and drawing of a plan is an objectivation of the mental images of an architect, as is the construction of the building by those whose job it is to objectify the building from the plan.

Somatic structures are, for the most part, constructed during intra-uterine life, childhood and adolescence. They are maintained throughout the whole of each person's lifetime.

Psychic structures are also constructed from the beginning of life (the very first cell), but the psyche never stops growing because each person, by learning, adds new things to it in the form of new functionings. To know how to surf does not preclude or displace learning to ski. Our muscles are polyvalent. In Gattegno's model, the putting into place of a new functioning is an objectivation.

## Passion

Passion is the attribute of the self that mobilizes energy for a long enough period of time and with sufficient intensity to bring to completion any project one has given to oneself.

Passion is the mark of what Gattegno calls "absolutes". At certain periods of each life, we become passionately interested in some aspect or other of the world in which we live. The object of the passion tells us which absolute any individual is in at any particular time of his life. (See Chapter 4.)

Passion is also found in projects of short duration. In education, its presence informs the teacher as to whether an exercise she has proposed is well adapted for a particular student. When children continue to work beyond the bell or even throughout their break, passion is clearly present. Like concentration, then, passion is an indicator for teachers which enables them to gauge the effectiveness of their teaching.

## Adaptation

The fact that we do adapt to the world and accept others for what they are shows that the self knows that there is an outside reality which is what it is and which constrains us in uncontrollable ways. In areas in which I am not in control, it is unwise to pretend that I am. Babies show that adaptation functions from the start. But even in some small children this attribute can become dulled in some circumstances and if this continues, non-adaptation can turn into an unfortunate trait of personality.

In those societies which are in the social absolute, teachers, especially those working in kindergartens and primary schools, are given the task of making children more tolerant and adapted to society. The adaptation we are discussing here is broader. It is our adaptation to everything we may have to live, whatever happens in the future.

A teacher can work in such a way that this attribute is enhanced rather than dulled. In a language class, once students have made a sentence, asking them to reformulate it in a variety of registers requires of them that they adapt. Looking at mathematical situations from all possible angles contributes to keeping the faculty of adaptation active. In fact, if a teacher works deliberately so that her students must keep their selves at the helm, this attribute of the self will be solicited. Adaptation will remain easy for them.

## Learning

One of Gattegno's major propositions was that "Learning is becoming aware". Everything that I learn is the result of an awareness and, as we saw earlier, awarenesses take place constantly. As we shall see in Chapter 5, when the self is at the helm then learning takes place.

Learning is the word given to processes by which the self changes itself over time. It does this as a result of its contact with the outside world, or by becoming aware of inner movements of energy. Thus the domain of learning includes subtle transactions taking place within the mind.

In the classroom, I know that each student can learn since all without exception have demonstrated their capacity to do so on many occasions: in learning motor skills, social skills and the complex abstractions involved in learning to talk, for example. If I know how to work with all the mental powers of my students, I know that all of them can learn what is being demanded of them. If some do not manage to do so, I must ask myself if the challenges I am proposing, or my ways of proposing them, are satisfactory. Am I in touch with their reality or am I imposing my own?

It is not because I teach that they learn. Indeed, there is no necessary link between the two activities, which take place within two entirely separate human beings. So it is my responsibility to find a way of teaching that ensures that learning will take place within my students.

Learning is the subject of Part 2 of this book.

## Characteristics of the attributes

All these attributes are present from the beginning of life. To educate myself is to give myself new skills, new knowledge, and so on, but it is also - and usually more importantly in the long term - to educate my self; and this is equivalent to saying that I am improving the functioning of its attributes.

When my self is at the helm, those attributes needed for dealing with the particular situation I am living will become more prominent. As the situation changes and I change with it, so the mix of attributes which are manifest changes, too. In our study, however, we can choose to stress just one attribute at a time while ignoring the others, in which case it gains a heightened relief and can become the object of the scrutiny of awareness.

Identifying, naming and describing attributes of the self, as Gattegno did, does not mean that the self itself is made up of discrete modules. Just as political, physical, transport and population maps give different lightings on a single underlying reality, so the identification of the particular qualities that Gattegno called attributes does not mean that the underlying re-reality of the self is in any way disunited. A written description may imply this, but it is not what Gattegno proposed.

It is a common observation that it is not the knowledge that one learns at school that will serve one in later life - this fades quite quickly - but the training of the mind that one has gone through. Teachers and other educators can and should place this insight at the centre of their thinking about education. In the classroom, it is possible to work in such a way that the teacher deliberately uses the attributes of the self of each of her students, working so that they continue to develop the powers of the mind that have served them so well up to now. This, rather than the acquisition of knowledge, is what Gattegno would describe as a good education.

**Further reading**

A Working Model for Health – *Newsletter XVI.2-4*

*The Mind Teaches the Brain*

*The Science of Education*

*The Universe of Babies*

*Les forces psychiques qui nous aident*

# 3   The psyche, affectivity and the soma

As we said in the preface, Gattegno set about reconstructing all human activity in terms of energy. When he examined human beings in this light, he found it useful to distinguish energy in three states, which he described as free, locked-in and residual. He then made one further distinction: between residual energy that is associated with the past and residual energy directed towards the future. These four types of energy were sufficient for him to shed new light on what it is to be human while giving the discoveries of natural science their rightful place in his model.

**Free energy** is another way of describing the self.

**Locked-in energy** is the energy that is committed to the organs and tissues of the body. Energy can be locked in to different degrees. The energy of bones is so completely locked in that they may last for centuries after the death of the person who created them. Locked-in energy is another way of describing the soma (loosely, 'the body', but discussed below).

In the embryonic stage, whenever the self creates some somatic tissue and sets it to function, it leaves behind more energy than the energy it has locked in. The role of this **first form of residual energy** is to supervise what has just been constructed and to alert the self if a dysfunction occurs. This arrangement leaves the self free to move on to other activities. The residual energy left behind by the self as a means of indirect supervision is what Gattegno calls the psyche[6].

Since the self is continuously creative, and has a continuous need to be free to meet the unknown of every day – whether this is the creation of a new organ, learning to skip, or waking up one morning as a retiree after many years of work – there is a continuous need for the psyche to look after everything the self must leave behind as the self moves on to new unknowns.

---

[6] See Appendix B for a note on the psyche as an energy.

The residual energy left behind is of a different nature at different times in a person's life: somatic functionings in the early embryo, then automatisms and know-hows from the womb and childhood onwards, and also habits and social skills, prejudices and preconceived ideas.

As the self lives its life, changing time into experience, all it encounters and delegates to the psyche becomes the person's past. The psyche continues to grow and become more complex throughout one's life.

The **second form of residual energy** is called affectivity. It is the energy which is used by the self to mobilise the soma to meet what the immediate future might require.

> Affectivity is residual energy in contact with the future: the psyche is residual energy in contact with the past. (1978b:39)

### How does the psyche support the self?
The psyche's function is to maintain everything that has been put into place by the self from the start and up to now, as an integrated whole and in good working order. The psyche holds our functionings - cell division or digestion, for example - and our automatisms - speaking a language, skiing, riding a bicycle. It holds standard responses to the momentary or longer events of my life which do not require the intervention of the self.

> I have lived in Besançon for many years. Now I am walking down la Grande Rue, talking to a friend in English. Walking is being provided by my psyche, as it has been for almost all of my life. Talking, too, is furnished by my psyche, as it has been since I learnt to speak English as a child. I know I am in la Grande Rue because I have a host of mental images overlaid one upon the other so that I can access not only la Grande Rue as it is now, but also as it was at different times over the years. I have built up this stock in my psyche from the countless times I have been in this street over a thirty year period. I know what shops are where, so I know as I walk that the next one will be the bakery, the following one a bank, and after that, there is a clothes shop and then a shoe shop.

> I have just had lunch, and my digestive system is dealing with what I ate without my self having to intervene. My kidneys are doing their job, as are my lungs, my circulatory system and all the other physiological systems which are functioning at this moment.

> I am talking to my friend. My psyche is providing the words I am saying as I express myself in one of the two languages I can use with this per-

son. I have known her for many years and know her well, which is equivalent to saying that my psyche holds very many images of her in many different and varied contexts, some of which I can recall at will.

These three paragraphs describe the work of my psyche at this moment. I could of course have made the list of what my psyche is doing much longer.

However, at this moment in la Grande Rue, my friend and I are talking about an incident that happened yesterday. I am choosing the exact words I need to make my friend as aware as I can of what I have in my mind. This last sentence describes what my self is doing. I am, or it is, in touch with the feelings that the incident now engenders in me, in touch with the mental images underlying what I want to say (these images are held by my psyche), and in touch with what my psyche informs me about my friend. I am trying to balance these three to arrive at the most adequate expression of my thoughts and feelings for the singular person that is my friend. At this moment, my self is responsible for choosing the content of what I am going to say; my psyche mobilises the words and all the automatisms necessary to speak; my affectivity furnishes the energy required for this small project, the sentences which will occupy my very immediate future, and with these energies functioning together ... I respond to my friend.

The role of my psyche here is to furnish everything that I need from my past for me to live the present moment. The role of my self is to meet the unknown - in this case how best to make my friend aware of the situation and to move us in the direction of a suitable outcome.

> I am sitting at a table in a restaurant, eating fish. Since I grew up in a family in which fish was rarely eaten, it is rather a new experience for me. Suddenly, I become aware of a bone, tucked up high against the skin of my cheek. This is another way of saying that my psyche has drawn my self in, so that it is aware of the situation and becomes vigilant to the possibility of harm. My presence shifts instantly from the conversation to the site of the problem. My tongue moves round in my mouth for an instant, and suddenly, the bone appears, pointing outwards between my lips. I take it with my fingers and put it on my plate. My mind is already back with the conversation.

When I started eating fish, I learnt over the period of a few months to find a bone with my tongue wherever it might be in my mouth, to move it to a central place, and to rotate it in such a way that I could eject it a controlled distance out between my lips. And I then left all this with my psyche, which now holds this particular motor skill and furnishes it whenever it is necessary. I can certainly marvel at the extraordinary dexterity of my tongue, but marvel, too, that my self need no longer involve itself in doing this; that my psyche has completely relieved me of this task and of countless similar acts which would otherwise preoccupy my life.

> I am doing the washing up. Each time I handle an object, my psyche furnishes me with the correct pressure to apply for the object in question. I pick up a wineglass and am aware of how thin the bowl is. From this moment until I put it down, my self is mobilised. The light pressure I exert on the surface reflects my fear of breaking it. I wash it carefully and my self checks the sparkle and decides it is clean. As I put it on the rack, I monitor the distance still to go until it makes contact, so that I place the glass exactly where I want it, in the careful way I wanted to do so. I decide to dry it before I go on. Now I start on the plates. I take one and wipe it with the sponge. I then pass the fingers of my right hand round the plate and become aware of a small area which isn't smooth. I take the sponge and give the plate another little rub. My fingers tell me that this time the plate is clean. I place it on the rack, do the rest of the plates and then pick up and wash the first saucepan. The way I then place it on the rack is very different from what I did with the wineglass I washed a few minutes before.

I have washed up countless times and my psyche provides me with everything I need for this. I am present only when necessary. How much presence I need for washing up depends on what I am cleaning. I was wholly present to the wine glass, less so to the plate, and while cleaning the saucepan I was present to my plans for the evening and my psyche took care of the job. I was minimally present with my fingers to assure myself that it was clean.

If I am learning to windsurf, I bring to this activity:

- gripping, which I first learnt while I was still in the womb (like all new-born babies, I could grip when I was born);

- standing, from my first year;

- leaning and swaying, from the same period;

- a highly educated sense of balance, which I started to give myself as a baby.

I developed my balance over many years: by learning to run in large and small circles, discovering that if I leaned inwards then gravity would help me to keep turning; by swinging myself around posts; by learning to ride a bicycle; by doing cartwheels; by skipping; by feeling the effect of acceleration on my soma as our car went round bends a little too fast, much too fast, or not too fast ...

In this learning experience of windsurfing, I will use all I can bring as a person with years of experience.

My psyche grows every time I add something new to it. Gattegno said many times, "The psyche grows, the self evolves."

## Affectivity
When I start saying a sentence, what energy holds it together until I get to the end?

It isn't my self; my self is an energy but has no extra energy to spare or spend. It isn't my psyche, the energy which has been left behind to look after my past and to give me access to it. It isn't my body, my soma. But we do reach the end of sentences, the end of football matches and people do survive through natural disasters. Gattegno named the energy required for living the present and the immediate future, affectivity. Affectivity is energy which the self can 'affect' or allot to sustain its projects.

What one feels of one's being when one is engaged in self observation is in fact both the self and the affectivity it has called in. Although the self is energy, it needs a source of energy in order to amplify itself if it is to affect its inner or outer environment. Affectivity furnishes the self with this energy.

In its usual use, the word 'affect' refers to emotions. Emotions and feelings are both part of affectivity as Gattegno uses the term, but are only particular examples of how this energy is manifest[7].

## The relationship between the self, the psyche and affectivity
In the present moment, the self, the psyche and affectivity function together. The self is in contact with a problem. The self has no spare energy,

---

[7] Gattegno sees feelings as abstracted out of emotions, and sentiments as abstracted out of feelings. Emotions are fleeting coagulations of energy, arising on the spot in response to our encounters with reality. Feelings are found in emotions, but are states of energy rather than amounts. After an emotion has gone, I can still evoke the feelings I had but without the energetic charge. Sentiments such as honesty, loyalty, integrity and patriotism, are on a third tier: attributes of feelings that are more abstract and intellectual, i.e. lightweight tokens which the self can easily entertain. (Sentiments can, of course, easily be amplified back into feelings and emotions.)

but the psyche and affectivity are at its disposition. The psyche can mobilize all the experience of the past to find a pre-existing solution to the problem. ("All the experience of the past" includes the soma, the earliest of the self's constructions that are now maintained by the psyche.) Affectivity is the energy which allows the self to act and remain engaged with the problem until a solution has been found.

Ideally, I would live my life oriented to the future with my self at the helm. My self is equipped for this endeavour in three ways. Firstly, by its attributes, which singly and in combination give me many ways to engage with the unknown. Secondly, by my psyche, which is supplying instant by instant whatever is useful from my past. Thirdly, by affectivity which supplies energy to the moment.

When my self is at the helm, the passage of time may be barely noticed and my psyche supports me in every way, freeing me to be completely with the task. I am alert, aware, concentrated ... As the moment demands, my self manifests one or other of its attributes to deal with the present, which I experience in a continuing feeling of freedom.

However, my psyche sometimes makes its presence felt. If I don't realise or acknowledge that a situation I am living is new, I meet it with my psyche, as if the situation were known and previous responses to it were adequate. At such a time, in Gattegno's terminology, I am being lived by my psyche. This is often the case when students are learning a foreign language. For example, if they don't realise that the sounds in the new language must be treated as new and must be learnt, they use what their psyche presents to them, the sounds of a language they already possess, and speak with a foreign accent.

It is usual for at least two generations to live together, and this, too, can lead to the psyche exercising inappropriate influence. For example, children sometimes live disturbing experiences which are beyond their ken. If my parents separate when I am four, what can I make of the situation? At this age, I have no understanding of the nature of the relationship they entered into when they came together, the reasons why they have parted and my place in the situation. I may well draw unwarranted conclusions about human relations which become part of the experience that is my psyche and which colour the rest of my life.

To 'get out of bed on the wrong side' is a sign that one has one's psyche at the helm. On such mornings, the quality of my life is viscous and I am aware of the weight of my psyche. My morning has nothing of the lightness I experience when my self is at the helm.

A teacher is being lived by her psyche when she responds to a real or imagined misbehaviour by thinking something like, "Oh Kevin! He's always like that." This teacher is now no longer seeing Kevin as a person, but has allowed her psyche to create a version of Kevin which leaves no room for Kevin to evolve, which, as a human, he is bound to do. Kevin, in turn, sensing that he has been branded, might well respond by meeting this teacher with *his* psyche whenever he is in contact with her ...

## Adherences, abscesses and heaviness
The psyche may contain more permanent dysfunctions: an 'adherence', a 'psychic abscess' or a 'psychic heaviness'.

'Adherences' limit the extent to which we live our potential as humans. To be French, Japanese or American is a fact of life. Everyone is born somewhere on the planet. To be proud of one's nationality is an adherence. One is less human if one is proudly French than if one is simply human. When people identify with the groups to which they belong (social, religious, political, scientific, etc) they constrain their behaviour to what is appropriate as a member, and thus are lived by their psyche in this area of their lives.

> I am eating with Isabelle. I watch her hold and use her knife in a way which my mother told me was 'bad manners'. I am aware of a movement in me which judges Isabelle and finds her wanting.

As a student of the psyche, however, I am also aware of the disappearance of the lightness I know I am capable of living at other times. This tells me that my psyche is now at the helm, adhering to my mother's model of good manners. A moment's reflection then tells me that Isabelle is certainly behaving in what is for her a perfectly appropriate way, and that it is only my psyche which is telling me that my mother's way is superior. (And everyone knows that mother is always right!)

Similarly, when people desire to impress others, rejecting the status they think others give them, they adhere to an image of themselves which fetters the self.

Since we live in society, from a young age we adopt the ways of thinking of our immediate environment, thus creating adherences. It is always possible, if the self is at the helm, to extract the energy from an adherence and from then on to respond in a way which is properly adapted to the circumstances.

> I am sitting at a table in a restaurant, talking with an acquaintance, Co-
> lette. During the conversation, I become aware of a small but growing
> distance between Colette and me. I realise that an opinion I have ex-
> pressed has ruffled her in some way. The conversation becomes a shade
> more distant. The encounter with Colette loses its lightness, and be-
> comes 'sticky', or even heavy.

Now I have a choice. I can confront the problem by speaking to Colette
about what has happened, trusting her to put her self at the helm, or I can
make a mental note to avoid this subject whenever I am with Colette.

Looking back, I can see that my psyche as well as hers met in this moment; however at the time my psyche was quick to tell me that the
problem was Colette's. I knew my opinions were more valid than hers (obviously, since they were mine), so I knew she was wrong... My psyche had
taken over this part of my life, and was dictating how I should live it. This
was an adherence.

As I become more aware of this behaviour of mine, I can become more
watchful, ready to put my self at the helm when I realise it is not.

'Psychic abscesses' are a second dysfunction. These can be places where
the psyche spends considerable energy to maintain an image to others,
perhaps dictated by local moral standards. A so-called 'skeleton in the
cupboard' might produce such an effect. To the extent that someone's
shame dictates his relationship to others, he cannot be as human as it is
possible for him to be.

The term 'psychic heaviness' describes those areas in the life of a person
where his self has abdicated and he no longer directs parts of his life, leaving decisions in the hands of his psyche. This person is lived by his
reactions instead of responding to the situation, to what is new. (Gattegno
made a clear distinction between reactions and responses. A reaction is an
automatic, unconsidered reply, coming from the psyche. A response takes
place when the self decides how it will reply.)

> Indeed, because our psyche is residual energy engaged in the contact
> with the past within our individual soma, it can come to the conclu-
> sion that the known reigns, that there is security in the stability of the
> somatic equilibrium, that the closed system of the psyche-cum-soma
> is all there is. When this view obtains the future has no right to be it-
> self; it becomes the locus of projected wishes and desires, the froth of
> the psyche functioning in conjunction with the imagination. Pre-
> humans live the life of the psyche and do not truly engage in a dia-

logue with the unknown. Hence, the pre-human future is mere extrapolation, is mortgaged in advance. "Ask for" seems permissible because it is no different from living outside true consciousness, and means living in the unrolling of days that are best if they are like happy yesterdays. (1975a:111)

## The role of sleep

Gattegno proposes that humans have two complementary states of consciousness, the waking state and the sleeping state. When I am awake, I engage in many activities of my choice, but I am also affected by what the people around me are doing, bombarded by all sorts of things which may or may not have meaning for me, some of which may put me out or even hurt me. Thus, I am not in control of much of what reaches me. Over the course of a day I accumulate my reactions and responses to what I have lived, and my awarenesses. During sleep, I shut off my access to the environment and open myself to all that I am inside, very much more than I am aware of in the waking state. (In Gattegno's model, my self has access to all of me during sleep, including access to what in other models is called the unconscious.) The reason why I sleep is to integrate all that I have lived during the day and to restore the balance of my energies in me.

During the waking state, I may have been slighted by an acquaintance, wilfully or not. For the rest of the day, I have in my mind what was said or done; it comes and goes all day. During my sleep, my self can extract the energy out of the emotion of the hurt, and when I wake, if I think about the incident at all, I am aware that the hurt has faded. The words might remain, but the energy of the emotion has gone. This is one of the jobs done during sleep.

I also wake physically refreshed, of course, having 'rested' or 'restored myself' which is another sense in which I have restored the balance of my energies.

When I have 'flu, my self does what it can to deal with the problem during my sleep, and the next morning I wake up feeling better. It may take a few nights' sleep for my self to treat the problem completely. If so, I stay at home, spend the day in bed and sleep more than usual.

During my sleep, my self can also inject energy into the awarenesses which took place during the day. During the waking state, I perhaps became aware of some little nothing, barely noticed out of the corner of my eye. Once I am asleep, my self may recognise that this was in fact an important moment of the day, and it injects energy into the awareness so that it is now retained in my psyche with the significance it merits.

In a similar way, the period of sleep allows my self to evaluate the episodes of the preceding day. If I meet someone new, our time together is likely to be rich in the exchange of factual information and I am largely occupied by this activity. It is only the next day, after I have slept, that I definitely know what I think about this encounter, whether I do trust this person or not, for example.

During my sleep, all that I am is available to my self, and is checked and balanced. All my systems and functions are brought up to date. "[The self] gets engaged in the jobs of sorting out, of analysing, of synthesizing, of discarding and so on." (1986 XV 3-4:12)

Every time I sleep, what I have lived during the day becomes a new foundation on which I rebuild all I have been in the past into a new whole. This last day lived is not integrated into all that I have been. The old does not integrate the new. Instead, the new integrates the old, recasting it to take into account all that I am now after having lived the preceding waking hours.

All that I am, then, is recast in terms of what the day has brought me. In this way, I can account for conversions, for the changes in me that happen at what we call defining moments. Every so often, I live a day which will change the course of my life. One such day, another child brings a skipping rope to school. Until now, my life has revolved around hopscotch. Tonight, hopscotch will disappear from my life. Now I live to skip. During my sleep, the energies I committed to hopscotch will be recovered, leaving in place only the know-hows generated by my learning to play hopscotch. Now, my self will invest its energies - physical, psychic and affective - in skipping. Over the days and weeks to come, I'm aware while I skip that I am getting better at it. All I learn during the hours I skip each day will be finally and fully automatised during that night's sleep. Since both hopscotch and skipping involve among other things a more robust sense of balance, this improvement will be there for me a few years later when I learn to ride a bicycle and again many years later when I take up windsurfing.

Conversions of many types, both bigger and smaller than hopscotch, occur in people's lives and all demonstrate that the new integrates the old. Some, of course, have implications for the whole of one's life. In 1971, I decided to go to a seminar on language teaching given by somebody called

Caleb Gattegno that a friend had said might be interesting. My knowledge of French was very basic, and I didn't understand much of what he was talking about. However, he gave a demonstration lesson in Chinese. This demonstration lasted one hour, and changed my life. From that moment, I absolutely wanted to be able to teach like that.

Since in this model the new integrates the old, the psyche is not a simple accumulation of all that makes up my past. On the contrary, each time I sleep my self has the opportunity to rework my psyche in the light of my most recent experiences, creating the new person I will be the next time I wake up.

These ideas will be revisited in Chapter 8, on memory.

### The soma

Gattegno defines the soma as,

> ... the live set of cells, tissues and organs enclosed in one 'bag'[8] and animated by the energy of the self. ... The presence of the energy of the self separates the soma from what is called body, which it becomes when considered as part of the material universe. (1977b:61)

The soma, then, is the equipment each person gives himself for living a life somewhere on earth: the physical part of the systems which allow us to know ourselves, to exchange energy in all the ways that are necessary to support life, to move, to perceive, to transport ourselves, to understand what the environment consists of, and so on. This equipment is usually called the body, but as Gattegno explains above, he makes a distinction between this and the soma. At death, the soma becomes a body, no longer a set of instruments of the self[9].

For Gattegno, the fact that the first job that the self undertakes *in utero* is to build itself a soma, and also that it is only through the soma that the self can manifest itself, demanded that he express the relationship between the two not as, "I have a soma" - and even less as, "I have a body" - but as, "I am a soma."

---

[8] Gattegno often spoke of "the bag", the container formed of the skin enveloping our body, in which can be found everything we carry around with us when we move. "In our bag are placed our bones, muscles etc. as well as our feelings, thoughts, experiences." (1977b:62)
[9] The conventional definition is that the soma is the body excluding the germ cells, but Gattegno used the word 'soma' as described here.

## The self and the energies of the soma

The soma gives the self the means both to move energy and to detect movements of energy. By design, we can detect energy entering through our sense organs and energy moving inside the bag. This does not mean that everyone can consciously feel everything that takes place inside, but rather that our whole being is constructed so that it can respond to minute parcels of energy, generated by ourselves or coming in from outside.

Without a doubt, we can educate our self to be more sensitive to our soma and to our environment. To some extent, this sensitivity is cultural.

> I had recently arrived in France and was sitting in a café with some French colleagues about an hour after the midday meal. Suddenly one of them said, "I'm really having trouble digesting those tomatoes we had for lunch." I was amazed that after a meal in which tomatoes were only one of many elements, someone would actually be able to detect in her digestion what it was in particular that she was having trouble digesting.

Over the years, I became aware that many French people have kept a proximity to their digestive processes that I, as an Anglo-Saxon, had lost. I began to explore how to regain contact with what was happening while I was digesting, and now if there is a problem with my digestion I almost always know what it is. I also know much more about how my choice of food at midday influences my well-being for the rest of the afternoon.

The ability to re-enter functionings that have been automatised for many years and with which conscious sensory contact has been lost is illustrated in the discoveries made by Thérèse Brosse in India in the 1920's. Brosse, a senior doctor in a Parisian hospital whose work influenced Gattegno as we described in the Preface, was amazed to find yogis who could voluntarily change the rate at which their hearts beat, a functioning which up to then had been considered outside of conscious control.

## The collective psyche: civilisations and cultures

Gattegno considered that civilizations start with one person - Abraham, the Buddha, Jesus, Mohammed, among others - whose life and statements are testimony that he operated at a level of awareness which represented a spiritual advance. These leaders inspired others to follow them, and their messages became the terms on which the civilisations developed.

> Not all civilizations produced the Mahabharata or the Old Testament which still inspire men and women by the millions. But all civiliza-

tions operated by handing down to those who were born in them a body of doctrine that spoke straight to their gifts and was compatible with all the ways of knowing available to them. (1977a:61)

Each civilization generates cultures which may differ from each other in so far as they also integrate conditions on earth, which may vary from valley to valley. (1977a:74)

During the process of evolution, certain of the great apes became human by developing the capacity to be aware of their awareness, thus leaving what Gattegno called the realm of animals and creating a new realm which is not determined by instinct. (This will be dealt with in more detail in chapter 9.) But not yet knowing how to live entirely free, humans have followed the lead set by spiritual visionaries among them, and given themselves civilisations and cultures. These can, if necessary, play a role for humans that is not dissimilar to the role that instinct plays for animals, defining limits and limitations that almost all humans need until we all learn to live with our selves entirely at the helm. Civilisations and cultures are less constraining than instinct. This is demonstrated by the fact that some humans change cultures and even, occasionally, civilisations, in order to adopt another. It is unthinkable for animals to change their instinct in this way. A cat cannot become something other than a cat.

But cultures by nature belong to the social absolute. This is why, in Gattegno's model, they do not display the essentially human aspects of human beings. The social and the collective psyche develop each other. As we said above, to be French is a fact of life, but to be proud of being French makes a person less 'human' because he is thereby limited in his vision of humanity. These are psychic adherences - for some, psychic abscesses - which prevent people from seeing the human in all humans.


**Further reading**

*The Mind Teaches the Brain*

*Evolution and Memory*

*L'énergie et les energies* (the end of the second volume and the third deal with humans)

*Can I be Creative*

# 4   The absolutes

## Temporal hierarchies in the development of a human being

Nobody learns to run before learning to walk, nobody learns to walk before learning to toddle, and nobody learns to toddle before learning to stand. This is because skills have prerequisites and there are certain orders which have to be respected in all learning processes. Gattegno used the term 'temporal hierarchy' for any such sequencing of development.

This chapter describes a particular temporal hierarchy which Gattegno called the absolutes. An absolute is a wholehearted engagement with a field of study, to the exclusion of much else, which we embark upon as part of our self education. The absolutes normally take place in a specific order and each lasts for several years. Living each of these absolutes allows a human being to develop as a rounded person. Gattegno noted that a feature of the absolutes is the passion shown by people engaged in them[10].

To undertake this study of the stages a human passes through on the way to old age, Gattegno developed new ways of investigation. He asked himself questions like: "What is there in the life of each of us which requires our total attention at a particular age, which is vital for this age or for the coming years and which cannot be put off until later?" (1975b:1) And also: "What activities did I engage myself in at that age, the consequences of which are still with me, integrated and metamorphosed by my later experiences, but still recognizable by my self?" (1975b:3)

## The absolute of psychosomatic construction: the embryo

For Gattegno, three elements come together at the moment of conception: an ovum, a spermatozoon and a self. So if the self occupies the fertilised

---

[10] Passion was described in Chapter 2 as the attribute of the self that mobilizes energy for a long enough period of time and with sufficient intensity so that any project one has given to oneself can be accomplished.

egg, it follows that the attributes of the self are present in humans from the beginning of their lives, from the first cell.

The self employs what it finds there, including the information in the DNA, to begin to objectify itself; that is to say, to construct a soma. The self directs the operation. It begins with cell division and the creation of the morula which a few days later becomes the hollow blastocyst. The blastocyst moves towards the wall of the mother's uterus where it installs itself, thus making the energy of the mother available to it. A new stage can begin, for now the self has at its disposal all the energy it needs and can undertake not only division but also growth.

This is the beginning of the embryonic period which lasts about two months during which each individual creates all his organs, entirely by himself, composing their tissue from what he finds in his mother's blood. It is incorrect to imagine that the mother constructs her baby. He depends upon his mother, but he is autonomous in his functionings. The awarenesses that he has, the functionings that he develops and the automatisms he then puts into place, are all his own.

As well as this, if chemical products he does not need for his development pass to him through the placenta, he is the one who must eliminate them. To do this, the self must be a very accomplished chemist.

For Gattegno, as we said in the previous chapter, the psyche corresponds, event by event, with the history of the individual. During the embryonic stage, this history is that of the construction of the soma. As it is forming the different tissues and organs, the self leaves behind a certain amount of additional energy in the somatic structures it is creating. The role of this residual, or psychic, energy will be to maintain the correct functioning of the finished construction once the self has moved on to other tasks, and to ensure the harmony of the soma as a whole. The psyche informs the self in the case of a dysfunction it cannot handle.

The role of the self is always to be in contact with the new, which in this embryonic phase means wherever the challenges of construction are taking place moment by moment. During embryonic life, the 'new' is essentially somatic—the formation of new organs and new tissues—whilst the 'old' consists of what is already functioning. The new is a learning experience, an experience which requires the presence of the self.

In other periods of life, the psyche will take on other appearances, depending on the particular activities of the self.

**The fœtus**
The work of the fœtus differs from that of the embryo, although both are involved in sophisticated processes of learning. The embryo worked to construct itself somatically: generating organs, making them functional and giving itself human form. The work of the fœtus is to grow.

The fœtus lives its life fully aware of what it can be aware of, since awareness is an attribute of the self. It is aware of its soma and has active access to all parts of it, including parts that will later come to be considered insensate. It knows its various functionings in the most minute detail, including functionings that will later come to be considered involuntary. It is aware of its own chemistry and, as is increasingly recognised, aware of what reaches its senses from the outside world[11].

The fœtus is involved in many temporal hierarchies, some of which are very simple. For example, it cannot study certain things before being big enough. Thus in order to begin the study of the touch sensations its skin produces, it needs to be sufficiently big to keep itself in contact with the wall of the uterus. It is at about seven months that the fœtus can start to do this work, so that, after birth, the new-born can recognize the place on its skin where a fly or a mosquito has landed.

**The absolute of vegetative adaptation: new-born babies**
After the time spent in the womb, given over to the construction of the soma and its functionings, a baby is born and immediately begins a new series of learnings which correspond to what it needs to do in order to survive in its new environment. This period is the absolute of vegetative adaptation to the given environment, both natural and social.

The jobs undertaken are urgent. No baby can put off until later learning the mechanics and the chemistry of respiration, for example, nor those of digestion and elimination. Its life depends upon them. For it is one thing to construct one's lungs, and quite a different thing to make use of them for the varying levels of gas exchange needed for the metabolism of a new-born baby living a day of its life - asleep, awake, at rest, in motion, digesting, etc. Furthermore, these circumstances can include challenges that

---

[11] A.W. Liley (1972) described what the fœtus was wrongly considered to be until quite recently: "For many centuries interest in foetal life was restricted to anatomical studies by embryologists or to mechanical problems in delivery as they presented to the accoucheur. The legacies of this era are well known - particularly the attitude that, apart from some aimless kicking which began in the fifth month, the foetus was a placid, dependent, fragile vegetable who developed quietly in preparation for a life which started at birth."

evolution could not have prepared any baby for, such as breathing the polluted air of a big city or the rarefied air of a mountainous region. The chemistry of the oxygenation of the blood must be studied, optimised, and its regulation automatized.

Similarly, before birth, babies prepare a digestive tract designed to receive food. But after birth, each baby must learn to deal with what is given to it. Baby food depends on the beliefs of the group into which the baby is born and may or may not be ideal.

Some mothers can bear witness to the fact that sucking is not a reflex, and must be learnt. This may take just a couple of attempts or may take more. The baby must learn to suck, to direct the food to the back of its mouth, to eliminate air taken in, to digest the food taken in, to assimilate what can be assimilated, and to evacuate what needs to be evacuated. DNA has provided the baby with the 'plans' for constructing the system necessary for these activities, but the baby must make his somatic structures function and then automatise their functioning.

There are many things a new-born baby must learn to deal with to sustain life and this takes four or five weeks. During this time, when the baby is actively living its life, what is visible is that almost all of its time is taken up in sleep. The baby is in contact with itself at the deepest level.

### The absolute of perception: infancy
Gattegno found that two productive questions he could ask himself for the study of babies were, firstly, "When a baby has been fed, is clean, is not asleep, and is not crying, when it is lying peacefully in its crib, how does a baby spend its time?" and secondly, "What can babies do without the help of anyone?" These questions helped him to put himself in the place of babies, to experience the world as they experience it, and to work out the temporal hierarchies necessary for them to arrive at the competencies that we recognise them to have months or years later.

In adults, the fibres of the optic nerve and other sensory nerves are surrounded by a sheath of myelin, the fatty 'white matter' of the brain. This allows nerve impulses to move very much faster. When they leave the absolute of vegetative adaptation after the first few weeks, babies signal the end of this first period of life by myelinating their sensory nerves[12]. Once the nerve fibres have been insulated, the baby can begin to make a finer

---

[12] For an account of the first nine months that includes a description of myelination, see Scheibel (1997).

analysis of the energies entering its bag. Consequently, they now have a greatly enhanced awareness of the outside world through visual, auditory and other sensory systems. They can now move into the absolute of perception.

Seeing as it is found in adults, if we take this example, is not a given at birth. It must be constructed, and educated vision is so complex that it take several years to create. In learning to see, the infant must learn to master the muscles which direct each eyeball: for up and down motion the equivalent muscles of each eyeball are used, whereas for left or right motion the inner muscles of one eyeball and the outer muscles of the other must be yoked together. The infant will spend several months learning to control the tension of these voluntary muscles so that they function swiftly, precisely and in a coordinated manner. The opening and closing of the pupil must be mastered, so that the quantity of light that enters is regulated. The crystalline lens must be controlled so that the light striking the retina will be perceived as a focussed image. These activities and many others constitute the systems which correspond to 'seeing'.

> In order to know the content of space, we have to relate consciously to the alterations of our soma resulting from the state of the iris, the state of the lens, the optic muscles that have been activated, the part of the retina that is struck by photons, and the individual and collective quality of the photons. (1973:36)

The presence of awareness in this activity gives us another dimension, the learning which corresponds to 'looking'. In looking, the self makes itself aware of the effects when photons enter the eyes and learns to interpret the different forms that these take. The self must undertake a new education, a series of studies involving form, depth of field, colours, tints, the play of light and of shadow, and many other phenomena. This learning lasts for hours a day during the early life of the infant, the time it spends alone in its cradle in dialogue with itself, and continues to be actively developed until at least age five. The child has to objectify the mechanisms of vision as part of the general energetic dynamics of its soma.

> Suzette is wearing dark blue jeans. She is sitting on a chair with her legs crossed and her granddaughter is sitting on her knee. The child points to the cloth covering Suzette's knee and asks, "What colour is that?" "It's blue." She points to the bottom of a fold of material running from the knee cap to behind the knee, and asks "What colour is that?" "It's blue." She points to a ridge running along the top of the fold, and asks her grandmother, "What colour is that?" "It's blue, too."

Much of vision is learnt too early for there to be any verbal accounts of the process, but this child has noticed the shades a garment can take on in different lightings and has not yet decided whether she should ignore these changes or not. The language she is learning tells her how others have resolved this issue.

The auditory system is put into place at the same time as vision and is no less complex. Here, too, we find a double education: both what it is to 'hear' and what it is to 'listen'. Listening mobilizes the self in the interpretation of the sound waves which reach the eardrum.

### Learning the mother tongue

Gattegno divided language learning into two distinct parts which he called 'learning to talk' and 'learning to speak'. 'Talking' refers to what will become the mechanics of speech whereas 'speaking' concerns the learning of the mother tongue.

A few weeks after birth, once the urgent matters of his vegetative life have been dealt with, one of the first awarenesses a baby has is that there are certain things he can do with himself because he is now in a new environment: he is surrounded by air. He begins the series of activities which, although he of course does not know it, will culminate in him talking, which in turn will later support his learning to speak the language of his environment.

He begins experimenting with the different ways he can use his respiratory system to move air through his vocal tract while also playing with the sensations of flow, pressure and vibration that he can obtain by modifying the muscle tone of his vocal folds, tongue, lips and cheeks. It is clear that this job is essentially work on muscle tone and sensation because it is done by all babies, including the deaf.

A further opportunity to learn something new occurs when the baby becomes aware that the sensations are sometimes accompanied by noises that he can hear and realises that he is responsible for them. This discovery opens up a new world which he sets out to explore with all the passion that keen observers of babies know them to have. What the observers see from the outside is that the baby has begun cooing and gooing. What this means is that he has begun to undertake an investigation of the possibilities which are open to him because he is equipped with sound-making and sound-perceiving systems.

Here is how Gattegno describes some of this process:

The important point here is to grant to babies their ownership of such a presence, conscious presence, in the various organs composing the phonation system ... acting on one's tongue and one's larynx at the same time and studying their respective contributions to final products which encompass each of them separately and all the intermediate mixings of both. When lips are added, when the walls made of the cheeks, the palate and later the teeth, are called in, it becomes obvious that a whole spectrum of complex sound productions are available to every child who can then play variations on them. These are gratuitous combinations produced by the self mainly for its acquaintance with a given somatic system generated *in utero* and whose possibilities can only be known and assessed *ex utero* when air can flow through the organs under variable conditions proposed by the self for that study and ending in a thorough acquaintance.

Endless hours are spent by the young child not yet 10 weeks old, say, to make sure that learning has taken place, i.e. that a mastery has been achieved which might make possible other conquests than sound production. Vowels are produced first. But for each a baby has to find exactly how it is made in terms of quantities of energy poured (or simply added) in the relevant muscles in order to remake them exactly, thus leading to an awareness of sameness. Once this is attained a baby can act on the duration of the utterance and how the somatic meaning of that sound shortened or prolonged, [can be] reproduced continuously or staccato. An alternative, open to all, is to produce a different sound and recognize it as such by the amount of energy affecting the various muscle tones of the muscles involved. As soon as two sounds are known for what they are from within and hence how they differ, a possible exercise is the production of sequences of the two, intermingled in various ways. The 'algebra' present is acknowledged and leads to the awareness that, say, *a i* differs from *i a.* that *a a i* and *i a a* are not the same, but that *i a i* is unique and remains the same by 'reversal'. (1985:11)

Thus the infant integrates talking, hearing and listening. He can now increasingly both predict the sound that a configuration of his vocal tract will produce and the configuration necessary to produce a sound he envisages making[13].

---

[13] Here again, these are the forward and inverse models, and children develop similar paired models in many other fields of learning.

In the case of deaf children, once their investigation of the new environment of the air has taken place, they move on to other challenges. For
them, the exploration of their sound-producing system has been in terms
only of the tactile sensations that they can produce with it.

Because infants have not yet surrendered to the linguistic world around
them, they are not limited to what this has selected among all the possible
choices of sounds. This is why it is common to find children of about one
year of age who experiment far beyond what their community has retained
for its language. Some infants even invent a personal language, unique
and perhaps incomprehensible to the outside world.

## Learning to speak

Almost all the children who learn to talk also learn to speak the language
of their environment, even if this language is considered very difficult by
adult learners trying to learn it later in life as a foreign language.

Gattegno describes imitation as one of the factors that leads to learning
the mother tongue. Not, however, the imitation by the infant of the people
in the family circle, but the imitation by his family of what he is producing.
The infant talking in his crib happens to produce "ma ma" when his mother is present, and she willingly interprets this as him saying her name. She
says back to him the sounds he is producing as an expression of her pleasure and approval. His mother's imitation allows him to become aware that
she can say what he can say, and the result is now a "mama" that they
share. This awareness is the bridge between his inner exploration of the
sounds he can produce and the outer world of spoken language. It will
allow him to enter into the exploration of what will become his mother
tongue. It gives him a new domain to explore with questions such as:
"What can I hear, coming from outside, that I can already say?" and "Can I
say other things that I hear coming from outside?"

As far as the language of his environment is concerned, before this awareness he could only work on what was then accessible to him, that is to say,
the energetic qualities of the language: the intonation, the melody, the
rhythm, the volume and also the emotional state of the speaker. He now
moves into a new phase which is to make what he hears and what he says
correspond. In certain cases, he can manage to do it immediately. Words
such as "mama", "papa" and "dada" are easy for him. Other words allow
attempts which are more or less successful. Others again are much too
complex for the capacity to analyse that the infant has developed so far.

Infants do not initially teach themselves to talk and speak because of a need to communicate. They know very well how to tell their caregivers what they want without having to use language. To signal to an adult that "I've had sufficient, no more yogurt just now," an infant has only to turn his head away from the spoon and keep his mouth closed. The goodwill of the two partners is sufficient. The language, on the other hand, is learnt because talking and speaking are interesting activities that infants can engage in with what they have at their disposal. Later, the child will become aware that words give him a new power over the environment, providing an excellent reason to continue his engagement.

### The absolute of action: childhood

Around the age of five, children move into a new absolute, that of action. Action at this age becomes the primary way of knowing, a way of knowing not only the world but myself-in-the-world.

To undertake the study of boys and girls, Gattegno turned away from the data that is usually collected by observers of childhood. Instead, he asked questions including those already noted at the beginning of this chapter: "What is there in the life of each of us which requires our total attention at a particular age, which is vital for this age or for the coming years and which cannot be put off until later?" (1975b:1) And: "What activities did I engage myself in at that age, the consequences of which are still with me, integrated and metamorphosed by my later experiences, but still recognizable by my self?" (1975b:3)

For boys and girls of primary school age, the answers can be found in their intensive study of action. At that age, everything they encounter is seen for its potential for action: marks on the footpath are an invitation to play hopscotch; walls were built for climbing onto and walking along; floorboards give opportunities for stepping along thin lines heel to toe; trees are on this earth for the purpose of being climbed; the best way down a flight of stairs is to slide down the banister, and the best way up is two by two and soon after, three by three. Marbles, skipping, playing tig and dozens of other activities take up most of a child's free waking hours.

Once Gattegno had seen what children do spontaneously with their time, another question came up: "Is there so much to find out about action that five or six years are required from each of us even though we are most efficient learning systems?" (1975b:6)

He found that there was, for living the absolute of action is needed for a complete integration of perception and action into a functional pairing which will be available for the rest of our lives. Some activities put perception at the service of action, others put action at the service of perception.

During the previous absolute of perception, the self mastered the mechanics of seeing and automatised the motor and mental processes involved. However, this type of seeing is synthetic in nature, with the gist of what can be seen being apprehended immediately and the self then recognising details.

The self also discovers the many possibilities afforded by evocation. To evoke, it must produce detailed mental structures which require analysis of what is seen. Drawing is one activity that educates vision to this end. Almost all children in the absolute of action like to draw and paint. Here, action serves perception. Many drawings will be made of faces, people and houses because many of their details need to be investigated analytically. Questions of position, colour, texture, relative size, the distortions involved in moving from three dimensions to two, and many more must be resolved.

> [W]hen they are taught perspective, the young draftsmen will integrate a mental attitude with their sight and prove once more that drawing is a way of knowing sight as a mental instrument of the self rather than as an organ anatomically and physiologically endowed to see everything all at once. (1975b:20)

On the other hand, learning to throw is an example of perception serving action. Since we see with our eyes and we throw with our muscles, a learning process will be necessary to integrate the functioning of the two. Of course, children have thrown before, but what they discover now is different. Toddlers have learnt that throwing a piece of paper or a feather and throwing a spoon or a plate yield quite different kinds of results. Now, in the absolute of action, the job is to learn to throw at a target. Children become aware that the perception of distance can tell them how much energy to use in the throw. This involves putting together positional information provided by the eyes with the distribution and amounts of energy that must be expended in different muscles in order to reach the target; perception at the service of action. As skills improve, the games evolve so that they constantly remain a challenge which will deepen the learning.

> Would it be a game if there were no successive broadening of the challenges, each proving that the previous one had been mastered and was available to be taken on to the next? (1975b:32)

In marbles, for example, the first stage is to learn to flick one's marble beyond a line to within a certain agreed distance of the target marbles—perhaps the span of a hand or the length of a foot— in which case one wins the closest target marble. When this level has been mastered, the game is made progressively more difficult until at the end, it is necessary to fire one's marble so that the target marble is shot out of a circle, which itself becomes bigger as skills increase. When this last level is reached, the game of marbles ceases to interest a child and another game takes its place. However some of the skills developed in marbles can be transferred; for example, to throwing a ball to hit the moving target presented by other children running around.

Skipping involves the coordination of a movement made by the wrists and the arms with the act of jumping at just the right moment. Moving the rope is learned quite quickly, but it may take a day or two before the jump is regularly made so that the rope passes under the feet. From this point on, the challenges lie in speed and skill: two jumps between each passage of the rope, one foot after the other, two children skipping using the same rope, side by side or face to face, speed for the sake of speed. Another stage is reached when the rope is turned by other children. One challenge then is to enter without being caught by the turning rope. How many children can this turning rope accommodate? Can we turn two ropes at the same time but in opposite directions? How can one enter then? Here is an activity which presents challenges for months.

Most children who learned to skip have only very vague memories of this activity. This is because skipping was not, in fact, a social activity. The type of memory which remains is made up of complex muscular patterns built into the soma, an intimate knowledge of these kinds of movements and their consequences. Such games yield somatic behaviours rather than memories.

In parallel with this exploration of muscular action there is another way of engaging with the world which emerges at the primary school age - that of virtual action. A virtual action takes place entirely in the mind, in one's imagination. It is obtained by taking the energy of the performance out of a real action, leaving the intention and the prediction of its likely results. Thus a virtual action costs far less than an actual one. We discover that we can act virtually in a way which is in accordance with a physical action, and we know that the virtual action is a tracing of the physical one, experienced as a dynamic image. When we then learn that we can manipulate dynamic images at will, this opens the door to the worlds of imagination and fantasy.

Boys and girls of primary school age create and explore vivid imaginary worlds, co-opting into them objects from the real world that they use as props when convenient. Thus a stick can become a horse, a rifle or a sword, as required. This is why certain undefined objects can be used much longer than specialized toys.

> While a box can be used as a police car or an ambulance, the ready-made police car is that and only that; hence the request for more and more cars to meet the power of the imagination in contact with the unchangeable given. Whilst a sheet hanging down from a table turns the space underneath into the kingdom of a child where he or she can act out what he or she fancies, a furnished doll's house imposes its shape and its furniture (although it too can be used symbolically). (1988b:139-140)

Obviously, the passage to adolescence does not mean that actions disappear. What changes is that action is put to the service of what has to be learned during the absolute of adolescence. The law of subordination and integration (discussed in Chapter 9) works on a psychological level in the area of absolutes and will be found at work in this new absolute.

## The absolute of the inner life: adolescence

Adolescence is the period of life in which the self is in contact with itself as energy, when it studies many of its own attributes.

> The self ... sees that it is more than just its behaviours and the process by which it brings these behaviours into being. It sees itself as a participant in a dynamic energetic universe. To recognize oneself as energy is to become aware of what is in us other than objectifications. This new awareness is precisely what occurs in the adolescent activity of revising the content of one's 'soul'. While in the preceding period, every child only objectivated his means of action, now the individual examines his actions with regard to their energy content. In this change we see the fundamental difference separating the general behaviour of the boy or girl from that of the young man or young woman, a difference that is immediately visible to all. (1988b:211)

During the absolute of the inner life the self investigates emotions, feelings and sentiments. Adolescents give themselves opportunities, too, for the exploration of physical and mental pain by prolonging and intensifying pain in order to study it. This is mental gymnastics, more delicate than the muscular gymnastics we are familiar with.

Adolescence is the period during which one discovers friendship. It is during adolescence that one chooses a friend, usually of the same sex and the same environment but outside the family. During the preceding period, children use each other as partners to construct games requiring several players, but they only put up with each other for the time that the game lasts and are ready to break all contact and never speak to each other again on repeated occasions. During adolescence, on the other hand, friendship is the opportunity to encounter the other, to discover real sharing. It is then that one learns to make a place within one's self for the other, exactly as he or she is, and where one explores oneself through the presence of the other.

> When the child, who has created his frameworks of action, discovers himself as inner energy, his power of loving appears to him for the first time. He discovers 'the other' as a spiritual being and this discovery will shift the emphasis of his life so that it is lived under quite new conditions. (1988b:230)

At the same time, adolescents infuse their environment with spirituality. If the environment does not contain a religion, the adolescent sets up something else as an absolute. He may become passionately atheist or throw himself into poetry or music. If his environment does contain a religion, it is at this period of his life that he adopts it totally, perhaps even finding his vocation. For Gattegno, he is mistaking religion for spirituality; he is the one who furnishes the spirituality which nourishes his religion.

During adolescence, awareness of thought emerges. Thought exists at all times during one's life, but it is at this period that adolescents become aware of their thinking and try deliberately to express what they find in themselves using language. They write a diary or poems.

They also create their own logic for the first time:

> Insofar as it is distinguished from logic, thought is a spiritual, human functioning - that is, an expression of the self in its freedom. The adolescent gives us the proof of this freedom every day, by his refusal to think logically, by his lack of appreciation of logical constructions in the rational sciences, and by the use that he makes of contradiction to discover himself as energy. He creates no confusion in himself from the fact that some of his propositions are self-contradictory, and he can be perfectly loyal to two opposed ideas when they are set

out for him. This is an everyday experience for all those who live with adolescents. (1988b:226-227)

The absolute of adolescence is usually the time for puberty. For Gattegno, it is not puberty which triggers adolescence, but the exploration of oneself as energy which triggers puberty. An adolescent reaches puberty because he is capable of loving. Although love and sexuality are merged in our society, adolescents know the difference perfectly well. They are capable of exploring sexuality coldly without looking for happiness in it. Quite separately they wish their love to remain clean.

> In all climates the songs of love are similar, and the male student who sings parodies would never do so before a woman who moves him. For the adolescent, love is spiritual and love is pure because he has transcended the physiological in his adolescent experience. (1988b:233)

During childhood, while the child is in the absolute of action, it is advantageous to be small, to have one's centre of gravity placed very low. But at the beginning of adolescence, he will undertake a new exploration, that of his physical power. Now he can begin growing again. In his actions, he will put the accent on physical power rather than on the fineness or the precision of his movements.

## The absolute of the intellect
Once the universes of perception, of action and of the inner life have been explored, a young man or a young woman can move into a new absolute, that of the intellect.

When children leave primary school in the West, they receive an education based almost completely upon the intellect, with the result that when the absolute of the intellect would be naturally entered, they have often lost their capacity to be inspired by its contents. But for those who do not founder under the weight of their schooling, it can manifest itself; for example, as joy when contemplating the economy and elegance of the great systems in the different sciences, or by a feeling of exultation at the sight of the wealth of books bearing witness to human enquiry that are visible in a good library. "All this is for me!"

Now, young people find real pleasure in discovering the laws which govern natural phenomena. Parallel with this exploration of natural science, young people also undertake an exploration of the literature of their environment. Since authors often create caricatures of humans, and make them live emotional crises far more intense than those that most real humans have the opportunity of living, literature becomes an excellent way of continuing by proxy the study of emotions begun during the previous absolute. This study is now continued at a second level in the absolute of the intellect, using the analytical tools developed by the thinkers in the field of literature.

### The social absolute: being an adult in the twenty-first century

The concept of an absolute can be applied to a society as well as an individual. Western countries have been living in the social absolute for about a hundred and fifty years, since Auguste Comte invented the concept of 'society' and people then became increasingly aware that they could influence the society they lived in by creating groups.

Thus young men and women today come through a series of personal absolutes to arrive like almost all the grown-ups around them as adults in the social absolute. The exploration they now enter into may last for the rest of their lives. They will usually want to take their place in society: to work, to find a partner, to create a home and perhaps to have children. When the society in which they live is in the social absolute, all sorts of ways will have been invented to allow them to do this more easily and better than in previous times.

For the individual, the social absolute is characterized by his need to explore the different ways he can influence the group. This takes the form of joining or forming associations and organisations to promote or protect this or that, to defend the interests that are dear to him, and so on. On a personal level, he learns to find money using social means such as bank loans or payment by instalments. A few learn to group people together in order to create a company, the effect of which is to increase the riches of the group as a whole.

The whole of society has been learning to create and investigate new forms and structures. It is not by chance that the great social movements date from about a hundred and fifty years ago. Trade unions, associations of managers, protest movements - all aim to modify the society in which we live. Crèches, child minding centres and kindergartens have as one of their aims to socialize the children who attend them. Social inequalities are sought out and hunted down in primary and secondary schools and elsewhere. Associations of parents try to influence the behaviour of those whose job it is to make decisions in the area of education. Currents of all kinds flow through the ocean of society as people try to find ways of increasing their power or taking social action. In 1985, Bob Geldof, and then many people and very quickly almost everyone, suddenly found themselves unable to ignore the fact that people were dying of starvation. They found twentieth century ways of raising money to combat this: huge concerts simultaneously spanning continents. The most recent collective awareness is a social awareness and the ways of taking action are social.

Most of us are immersed in our society and in exploring the social absolute that our society itself is immersed in, so it is difficult for us to see that other ways of living a life are possible for us. We fit into our absolute so well.

## The absolute of relativity

Gattegno saw another absolute emerging, in which one could undertake a new exploration: the absolute of human relativity. To find oneself in the absolute of human relativity, it is only necessary to become aware that all of us are in absolutes corresponding to stages in our physical and psychological growth.

It is because a father lives profoundly in the social absolute that the 'antisocial' behaviour of his teenage son is so difficult for him to bear. For his son, the intensity with which he is exploring his emotions tells us immediately that he is in the absolute of his inner life. The word was not chosen by chance. Both live their lives of exploration in an absolute way. From a relative point of view, both are doing what they are doing for their own good reasons. Both are absolutely right! Relativity allows one to see the correctness of the two ways of living; each of them is living his life fully.

## Further reading

For the general theory:

*Vers une théorie de la rélativité humaine*

For individual absolutes:

*The Universe of Babies*

*Of Boys and Girls*

*The Adolescent and His Self*

*Know Your Children as They Are - A Book for Parents*

*La psychologie des petits enfants*

Oller D. (2000) *The Emergence of the Speech Capacity*. Lawrence Erlbaum Associates: Mahwah, NJ

# Part II

# How do we learn?

"Learning is becoming aware."

Caleb Gattegno (in countless writings)

# 5   About learning

Gattegno held that only awareness is educable. All learning takes place by means of either an awareness or a series of awarenesses. This means that the awareness becomes the conceptual unit of learning. The awareness is to education what the atom is to chemistry. Just as alchemy could develop into the science of chemistry once the atom had become its basic unit, so this proposition provides us with the means to found a new science, the science of education.

Gattegno further proposes that learning takes place in four stages: stage one, the basic awareness that there is a field to be explored; stage two, the exploration of the field; stage three, practice leading to mastery; and stage four, transfer.

He expressed this in different ways on different occasions. Here is the most informal:

> [L]earning, as a process, takes time, and is structured according to the three or four phases of
>
> – coming into contact with the challenge,
>
> – tossing it around to become more and more acquainted with it,
>
> – filling the gaps so that one gets on top of it, and
>
> – using what one has felt to have been mastered to enter a wider challenge, a new experience. (1982a)

In this chapter, we will start by looking at these four stages through a series of examples. We will then explore other aspects of the learning process which is, of course, not restricted to the learning that takes place in school.

In the following descriptions, some significant awarenesses are prefixed with an asterisk *. When it is useful to do so, we have added numbers which correspond to the stages of learning.

> In spring 1992, I was in a public telephone box in the Place Granvelle in Besançon making a phone call. At the end of the call, I hung up and turned to go out the door. I pushed on the glass panel and, as *it didn't open, I pushed a little harder. When *it still didn't move, *I realized [1] that I was trapped in the telephone box. Immediately, I turned my whole attention to the problem. I pushed again on the door, a little higher, *hoping that this would help. *Still the door didn't open [2]. I pushed on the door a little harder, lower down the panel, but *could feel [2] that there was no change in the resistance the door was offering to my hand. Then *I realized [2a] that this door was made, not of a single pane of glass, but of two tall narrow panels side by side. I pushed on the left hand side of the right hand panel and immediately *realized [2a] that there was more give in the door, that this was a more promising place to explore. I pushed a little harder, *trying to estimate [2] where the door was likely to yield most easily to my efforts. Then *I realized [2a] that I should push on the other panel as well. I did so and the door opened easily. I walked out of the box and went on my way.

This incident occupied only a few seconds of my life, but it can tell us about the four stages of learning as Gattegno saw them.

## Stage 1 – There is something to learn

The first and most basic awareness in a learning process is that there is an unknown to be explored. Until I realise this, no learning can take place. In the situation described above, the awareness numbered [1] corresponding to stage one, told me that I was in contact with the unknown. While I was still talking on the phone, I was not learning about the door, since I did not yet know there was something to learn.

## Stage 2 - Exploration

The unknown is explored through awareness. Since it is unknown, we may, and often do, make many mistakes. It is our activity in this stage which led many years ago to the recognition that we learn by trial and error. In the incident described above, after my stage 1 awareness, I immediately became involved in an exploration of this unknown, stage 2, using a three-step process:

a) I am aware of what is. This is necessary so that I can estimate what trial will be useful here and now;

b) I try a possible solution;

c) I become aware of the feedback provided by the environment, telling me the result of the trial I have just made. I use all that my psyche furnishes of my past experience to understand the feedback, and this puts me in a position to start this three-step process again.

Each trial and the feedback it provides allows me to make a new trial which I hope will be better adapted to the situation than the previous one. This is because I am already aware of the response of the environment to the previous trials and can adjust my trials one after the other as a result. This three-step process is used whenever we learn by trial and error, whether we are learning to windsurf, to make bread or to speak French. This is a very common process in our daily lives.

The awarenesses numbered [2] above illustrate this stage. Some awarenesses told me only that the current hypothesis was leading nowhere, while others were more encouraging and inspired a new and better adjusted trial, and thus hastened the learning process. In this case, the awarenesses numbered [2a] were more useful than the others because they led to more successful trials.

Learning happens through awarenesses, but the different awarenesses that contribute have different impacts.

### Stage 3 - The time to practise and automatise
Once an awareness of what is necessary has been reached in stage 2, we require practice in order to reach mastery. This is another way of saying that time will now be required for the construction of an automatism, once we know from stage 2 exactly what we need to automatise. We know that a particular learning process has come to an end when what we have learnt becomes automatic.

Over the next few months, I consciously looked at the doors of the telephone boxes I used in order to get out easily. Since I didn't use telephone boxes very often, this process took a long time but I gradually learnt to recognise one type of door from another, where to press and how hard. This became automatic.

**Stage 4 - The opportunity to transfer**
Whenever circumstances provoke a learning process that culminates in an automatism, we are then free in similar circumstances to spend our time otherwise, perhaps to meet a new unknown and learn something else. Everything we have learnt can be transferred, which means it can support other learnings or serve as a basis for more learning. Looked at from another point of view, every time I begin a learning process I have my previous learnings available to me. As we saw in chapter 3, this is because I sleep every night.

\* \* \*

I want to go to number 46 rue Henri-Monnier in Paris, a place I have never been to before. I know that I have to get off the Metro at St Georges because I looked this up the night before, and I come out of the station into Place St Georges, an oddly shaped square with several streets running off it. I look for a street name. The first I see is \*rue Notre Dame de Lorette. I consult my map of the city, \*find rue Notre Dame de Lorette, \*see that it both enters and exits the square, and \*realise that I should turn the map so that it corresponds to what I see from where I am standing at the exit of the Metro. Immediately, \*I become aware that rue Henri-Monnier should be a little further to my right. I go down to the corner, turn right and \*become aware that this is indeed rue Henri-Monnier. I look at the numbers on the buildings and \*become aware that I am in front of number 3. I walk up the street a few yards, look at the number on the next building and \*become aware that it is number 5. Immediately, since this is Paris, \*I am aware that number 46 must be on the other side of the street, further along. I look at a number on a building on the other side of the street and \*become aware that it is number 6. I walk past number 7... number 15... number 39..., checking the numbers on the other side of the street at the same time - number 16... number 38... When I see number 44, I \*am aware that I am very close. I find number 46 exactly where I expected it to be. I cross the street and go in.

This banal experience, which everyone lives so many times in their lives, illustrates the fact that some awarenesses are more important than others. The awareness that rue Henri-Monnier is on my right when I come out of the station is relatively more important than the confirmation that number 7 follows number 5. The awarenesses, when I see number 3 and then number 5, that the building I am looking for is further along the street and on the other side is more important than the fact that the building on the other side is number 16. However, the process of learning always consists of a series of awarenesses, on a continuum from the very small to the Eureka moment.

## Learning a foreign language

In a complex task like learning a foreign language, there will be countless examples of the four stages of learning. All the stages described in learning to open the door of a telephone box will be present, but they will overlap in time as different aspects of the language are addressed: sounds, meanings, structures, rhythm, intonation ...

In any one sentence that a student is saying, all four stages may be identified in different aspects of the production, and even in any one word several stages may be seen at the same time. Thus in a class of French students after 50 hours of English, when a student says "I have been living in Nice for twenty-three years," the situation might well be as follows. "Nice" is totally automatized, since the pronunciation is practically the same in English as in French. "I" has been used for many hours, and is probably moving towards the end of stage 3 or, for some students in the class, may even be automatized completely. The word "live" has been in circulation for many hours. It may be moving from the end of stage 2 to stage 3, or, for some students, already have reached stage 4. The word "twenty" is probably automatized from the point of view of pronunciation, but probably does not yet present itself spontaneously when required - we all know how hard it can be to count spontaneously in a new language. For "three" on the other hand, the pronunciation of "th" probably still requires a high level of presence - stage 2 - but the word may well present itself easily when required, a sign that, from this point of view, it has reached stage 3 or even stage 4. The construction 'have been + -ing' is brand new, dating from a few seconds ago, and belongs to stage 1. The student is just about to realize, or has just realized, that there is a new field requiring investigation.

Even if we examine the situation for just one student, it is highly complex. If the teacher of this class is aware of this complexity and can recognise each of the four stages of learning, which is not so difficult, she can work in different ways appropriate to the stages she detects in each learner for all the aspects of the language that she is working on.

## A more detailed example: learning completely new sounds

Here is an example of how a student learns a new sound in a Silent Way class, where the teacher will not provide a model for the students to imitate.

First of all, the teacher must make sure that the student realizes that there is in fact a new sound to learn. Once he has realized this, he can move to stage 2 as he tries to create the sound. Here, he works using feedback from the inner and outer environments as mentioned above.

He is dealing with two independent but closely related systems, the mouth and the ear, only one of which, the mouth, can be controlled voluntarily. All the muscles of the ear are involuntary muscles. The student can only will actions in the voluntary system. With his mouth, he produces a new sound which he hopes might be close to the sound required. He hears this new sound with his ears. Since he produced it with his own mouth, he knows that, muscularly speaking, his mouth was used in a new or special way and consequently he knows he should listen for a sound which is different from what he is used to hearing. He can probably predict at least to some extent in what ways the sound will be different from what he usually produces. He speaks here with the deliberate intention of doing something unusual and he listens to the result with the specific intention of hearing the unusual sound he has just produced, giving him two sources of feedback. He has feedback from his mouth telling him what it is doing, and his ears give him feedback about what changes they detect as a result. The teacher also gives him feedback, about how acceptable the sound is within the new language the student is learning, keeping his production at the exploration stage until the sound is correct. With these three sources of information, he develops both muscular and auditory criteria for the sound.

Once the student has managed to produce the sound to the teacher's satisfaction and to his own, he must practise it in a wide variety of different situations and contexts until he is completely at ease with it. He thus reaches the end of stage 3, when the sound has become completely automatized and the learning process for that particular sound is over.

## Human relations - getting to know people is a learning process

We would all like to keep our relations with other people fresh, especially relations with long-term friends. The four stages of learning give us a way of understanding how familiarity can be a danger if we allow our psyche to take over when our self should be at the helm.

I meet a new person - stage 1. I am aware that every time we meet can be a new opportunity to 'learn' both the person and myself in this relationship; whenever I take this opportunity, I am in stage 2 of the learning process. Obviously, if we meet often and over many years, my psyche will carry a huge quantity of information about this person, as it should. The danger then arises if I start to automatise our relationship – stage 3. Rather than this, every time we meet I can make room in myself for this person to have grown and changed, as he will do. In this case, I continue to explore myself and him - stage 2.

Using the concept of the learning process for human relations can be particularly helpful for our relations with people we live with. Having breakfast every day for 20, 30 or 40 years with the same person sitting on the other side of the table can lead to a relationship in which this person is no longer actually seen as a person at all. My self is no longer in contact with the self of the other. The relationship is now that of two psyches living in parallel, not two selves living together. Clearly when one reaches this point, reading the paper at breakfast engages one's self more than speaking with one's partner.

**The role of presence in learning**
I can recognize where I am with respect to each of these four stages by looking at what I do with my presence.

In stage 1, becoming aware of an unknown field changes what I am present to. I am now present to the situation that has captured me at that instant. Thus, in the episode with the telephone box above, I only became present to the door when I realized that, contrary to my expectations of how the world works, it would not open. Before that instant, I was still present to the conversation.

During stage 2, I am actively engaged in the exploration of the problem, and my presence stays with what I am trying to understand. Once I realized I could not get out of the telephone box, the conversation I had been engaged in vanished instantly so that I could devote myself entirely to the problem of the door.

During stage 3, my presence to the problem becomes intermittent, as I automatise more and more of my response. In our example, stage 3 would be indicated by a recognition, as I leave telephone boxes here and there round the town, that the box I am leaving is one of the two-pane kind, so that I have to push on the door in the particular place which will open it. I might even experiment a little with the best place to push in order to open the door with the least possible effort. There are other examples in the next chapter.

The end result of this stage is not usually noticed by people going about living their lives, since what characterizes it is that my response requires almost none of my presence in order to function. One day, if I am a student of learning, I might realize that I no longer even notice what kind of door the telephone box has. I just push in the right spot for the kind of door that it is. In the incident described above, the end of a stage 3 is illustrated in the casual way I initially pushed on the door before I first became aware that the door would not open. I had entirely automatized the way to open telephone box doors, this act requiring none of my presence, and this would have remained the case had France Telecom not decided to introduce a new style of door.

Stage 4 involves the possible transfer of what I have mastered. This skill is available to me in all I undertake throughout the rest of my life. It is experience, forged out of a series of experiences, which adds to my experience in this field. If opening doors has relevance some day in any of my other learnings, I have this experience to call on if required.

### Being present and paying attention
Once I become sensitive to my energies, it becomes possible for me to detect a distinct difference between being present and paying attention. When I pay attention, I am aware of spending energy in order to remain with what I am doing. When I am present, on the other hand, I have no sense of this. Here I am, reading a very good book. This costs me nothing. I am simply present to the book. Suddenly, I am interrupted because something else has to be done right now. I am aware while I am trying to engage in this new activity that it is costing me energy to remain with it. I am quite literally 'paying a tension': the cost to me is in the tension I must create to resist the pull of the previous activity. But as I let myself be drawn into the new activity, the pull of the previous one disappears and with it the tension needed to overcome that pull, and I become present to the new activity without tension which means that I return to a state in which the cost is zero.

### Presence and automatisms
My presence to the task is especially required whenever I am doing anything new or different. Gattegno cited the example of walking up a flight of stairs in darkness, an activity which tells us a lot about the work of our presence in relation to our functionings and our habits. When there is

light we rely on visual cues and climbing stairs is almost completely automatic for the able-bodied.

> It's dark. I feel around with my hands until I have found the banister and from the way it slopes I get an indication of the general angle of the stairs. I feel with my foot until I have found the first step and stand on it squarely. In order to move on to the second step, I lift my foot higher than necessary and lower it onto the step. By doing this, I discover the spacing of the second step from the first and I know, too, that I can rely on the fact that staircases are built with steps of equal height. After checking for a couple of steps that this staircase is indeed regular, and getting the height of each step well integrated into my feet, I can relax my vigilance.
>
> If I am with a friend, I can now go back to the conversation we were having before we began walking up the stairs, although I remain much more present than usual to the stairs, alert to any change which might take place. In fact, our conversation might very well turn to the subject of climbing these stairs in the dark. After a certain number of steps, or when I feel a change in the angle of the banister, I return all my presence to the stairs, in order to negotiate the top of the staircase correctly. I now progress step by step again.

Walking around your house in the dark is an excellent opportunity to study awareness and presence. We invite you to try it.

In a similar way, moving to a new home requires that we put into place many, many new automatisms which means that we must become present to all sorts of details in its arrangement. Is the door opener on the right hand side of the kitchen door or the left? Is it a knob or a handle? Is it easier to open with my right hand or my left hand when I come into this room? Which side of the door is the light switch on? What height is it? How far do I have to go into the kitchen in order to switch the light on easily? After a few weeks in the new surroundings, no presence is necessary for me to place my finger on the light switches. I use the most convenient hand to open the doors and it is always the same hand for a given door. The hand approaches the door at a particular angle, the best for the type of handle, and as it approaches, it is ready to seize the handle. All these actions have been integrated and become automatisms, stage 3 of the learning process. Indeed they are so integrated and automatic that sometimes when there is a blackout, I switch on the light even though I am carrying a torch in the other hand!

## Presence in practice and repetition

We can use the notion of presence to distinguish practice from repetition. Both involve reiteration. But a repetitive action can be accomplished without the doer being 'with it'. Assembly line work used to be a good example of this (think of Charlie Chaplin mechanically screwing bolts in 'Modern Times').

Practice, on the other hand, requires the learner to be present. At each trial he is present to what he is doing and aware of the feedback he gets from the environment, and he modifies his response as a function of this.

For the observer, the skier goes down the same slope ten times in the afternoon, because the observer, from the outside, sees the same thing happening each time. But for the skier, the slope is new each time. What must he do to negotiate this bump, not to fall in this bend, to lean at exactly the right angle at such and such a place? Each time the skier negotiates the slope, it is a different experience for him, because he himself is different each time, having accumulated the experience of the preceding runs. The skier is practising. He has no inner feeling of repetition. He knows himself to be working actively on the problem he has given himself.

As soon as he feels he has mastered a particular *piste*, which means he no longer needs to be present to it, he finds a more difficult one.

This distinction is as valid for a language or mathematics class as it is for an afternoon's skiing. Structures must be practised in each; however, drilling in a language class or rote memorisation of the tables in mathematics should be recognised as repetition and eliminated. They are not as efficient as ways of working in which the students practise what there is to be learnt without ceasing to be present and so falling into the inner state associated with repetition.

## Further reading

*The Science of Education, Part 1 Theoretical Considerations*

# 6   Learning experiences

One of the exercises we propose to those who wish to apply Gattegno's approach to teaching is to ask them to write an account of a learning experience. The student teachers are asked to choose something to learn which is not too complex and which can be learnt in a relatively short time. They are asked to observe how they learn while they are learning; studying and noting their awarenesses. The exercise has two aims: to learn to observe oneself as one is learning and to describe the process in detail in one of several ways which will be discussed further on.

What has been studied in this context is very varied: people have worked on learning to write with the left hand, learning to frame a painting, to belly-dance and even learning to keep one's house in order.

The examples which follow were chosen for their variety and because their authors have understood the role of awareness in learning and have been able to express this clearly. The examples describe the learning of sporting activities such as fly-fishing or wind-surfing, and manual skills such as calligraphy, throwing a pot and typing. In addition, demonstrating that to live is to learn, and to learn is often to change, some examples from everyday life have been included.

Some of the authors are less experienced than others in the observation of themselves as learners, but we felt that the variety of expression would be of help to the reader in recognising the processes involved.

There are several ways of describing a learning process. A learner can choose a very small part of the whole process, a representative moment, and describe it in great detail. In this case, what is being described is a singular learning process within another learning process on a much vaster scale. Or a learner may choose to describe what is being learnt from beginning to end, putting the accent on just a few key moments. It is possible, too, for a learner to write about the psychological difficulties which stopped him from making progress in the chosen discipline, and the way in which he set about going beyond these blockages. In the descriptions which follow, all three kinds of observations are represented. As in the previous chapter, awarenesses have sometimes been marked with an asterisk *, however in this case they were added by the writers (who may, of course, have missed some).

## Learning sports

First, we present some examples of learning recreational activities. They document the basic process of learning through awarenesses.

There are two descriptions of learning to windsurf. It is easy to see that although the activity is the same, the strategies and the awarenesses differ. Yannick Lorréard describes his first hour on a board. Pierre Stark is already a sailor and comes to windsurfing as an extension of sailing. He brings more technical know-how and writes in more technical terms. Pierre Stark's text is written in such a way that the four stages of learning are visible.

Although strategies differ, the learning process itself remains the same. It has often been said that every learner uses a different strategy in learning, and this is true here. But it is also true that every learner goes through the process described in the previous chapter; that is, series of awarenesses which can be placed within some or all of the four stages of learning.

As is always the case, the two men begin the experience of learning to windsurf having already acquired a wide range of skills that are prerequisites for this activity. They can both stand upright - they learnt this when they were children, as we all did - and they can hold things - this they learnt even earlier than standing, when they were babies. They have worked on their balance in varied activities over the years. And so on.

### Learning to use a windsurfing board
Yannick Lorréard, Besançon

Lying on the sand, I watched people windsurfing out at sea. I told myself: "They are lucky to be able to do that. I'd like to have a try." The next day, I watched them again; I felt it welling up in me until I said to myself: "Do it! There's no reason why you can't do what they are doing! Just try it!"

When I got to the place where they were hiring out boards, it took me only a moment to find myself with an hour of board-time ahead of me, and I didn't know what to do with it! I moved out into the water, but I could feel a kind of force which held me back. * There was a problem. I looked at the board more closely and realised * that the keel was scraping on the sand. The only thing I could do was to go out into deeper water, but where I could still touch the bottom. The water came up to my waist.

To get on to the board, I had to be careful not to fall. But the first time, it was not easy. When I was standing on the board, * I could feel little undulations of the water which made me lose my balance. Almost immediately, I fell. I had to begin again. Just as I was getting back on the board, * I noticed there was a rope on the mast. I hung on to it and then got onto the board. This rope let me gain my normal balance. But * I realised that to get the sail out of the water I had to pull hard on the rope. Pulling as hard as I could, * I became aware again that it was very difficult because the sail was underwater, which put pressure on it. I had to find a way of getting the sail out of the water. The only thing I could do was to pull, using all my weight, and, little by little, the sail came out and lifted. I could feel that if I pulled harder, it would fall on to me and I would lose my balance. So I had to pull carefully towards myself, letting the rope slip between my hands so that I could control my balance. I realised I was learning by trial and error, but I didn't really have any choice. No one was there to explain what I did or didn't have to do. My arms and legs were trembling but I was proud to be on the board. Then, with one hand, I caught the wishbone to direct myself while the other hand stayed with the rope. I glanced at the people around me and became aware that * I was moving along just like them. The hour was almost gone and I had to take the board back. This first contact was quite successful, in spite of all the trials and errors necessary to get to this stage in my learning.

## Learning to windsurf

Pierre Stark, Besançon

I am going to try to describe a learning process which took place 15 years ago. My memory of it is still very sharp, as I invested myself in it deeply, and even passionately. I have tried to put these memories together in a detailed way, but describing them as they remain in my memory.

This is only a part of the learning process of windsurfing.

1 - A field to explore!!

First of all, I discovered windsurfing after having sailed in boats for several years. It was an enormous surprise for me to see some foreigners (Dutch people) on this object which was even simpler than my boat! How could they do it without a keel, standing up? I watched them for a few days from my boat, and when they left the area a couple of days later, * I <u>knew</u> I would get hold of one of those things as soon as possible.

The following spring, I found what I was looking for in a sporting goods catalogue; I bought my first board by correspondence, having made up my mind that I would somehow manage to work out how to use one.

2 - The learning process: awarenesses and adjustments

After I had put all the pieces together like a puzzle on the shore, I decided to "jump in at the deep end", as it were.

I place the float in the water and * become aware when I put down the keel which touches the bottom, that I have to move away from the edge of the water if I want to push it right in. I prefer to push it in only half way so that I can get onto the board more easily.

I put the sail on the water and fix the foot of the mast on the board. * Ah, there are pockets of air under the sail and it doesn't sink.

I look for the direction of the wind because I know (a transfer of my experience of sailing) that I have to put myself between the sail and the wind if I don't want to get hit in the face when I pull it up. I set the board in the right direction as I would for my boat.

I place one foot on the board, in the middle; it moves a little. I get on, standing up. I am looking for my balance. I bend down to grasp the rope attached to the mast. * It is easier to keep my balance because I have something to hold on to.

I pull gently, then harder. * It is difficult to get the sail unstuck from the water. * I have to lean back. I pull harder, * the sail comes away from the water and I fall backwards. Why? Did I pull too hard?

I begin again, slowly, being careful, and * I feel when the sail comes out of the water that it loses its resistance. * I have to compensate by leaning less at the same time as the sail comes up. I have to "listen to it with my hands".

* After a few tries, I get it out of the water without falling. At this instant, I have no support because there is no resistance any more. On the contrary, * I feel the sail pushing me backwards! and I fall. I don't understand. * The wind has caught the sail. * I look around me: * my board has turned while I was getting it out of the water. I was so busy looking after the sail that I didn't realise it was turning. * So it is necessary to lift the sail and control the direction of the board at the same time.

And how do I control the board? * With my feet! I begin again, * giving all my attention to my feet. * Ah!, I would go more quickly if I took the cord in my hand before getting onto the board; and * I have something to hold on to there immediately.

I begin the whole thing all over again. I pull, looking at the board: * it turns a little as I push with my feet. * If I push with my left foot, it turns right and vice versa, that way I can control it. But that makes for a lot of things at the same time. I'm lucky the wind is light and there are no waves! At the moment when the sail comes out of the water I am still as unstable as before.

I have to find something solid to hang on to with my hands! * I pull the sail taut and it works! * I have something solid and I'm moving forward. (Pulling the sail taut to fill it and move forward and doing the opposite if I want to stop are things I know from sailing.)

* I feel myself pulled forward by a gust of wind. * I am standing on tiptoes. * I relax the tension in the muscles of my arms. No! * Not both arms! It's too late... * The sail has become too heavy and when it leans and falls, it takes me with it.

* I become aware too late that I can only relax the back hand to decrease the pressure of the wind, while keeping the mast vertical with the front hand, like a flag. * I also understand that I have to react very quickly. I don't have time to analyse the action. It has to become automatic so I won't be taken by surprise.

Later, I discover by trial and error that * pushing with the back hand and pulling with the front hand give the same result more efficiently.

3 - Automatisms:

A few years later, I can get onto the board, pull up the sail, leave and navigate while watching the clouds in the sky, the horizon (or even with my eyes closed!). I have completely integrated my body sensations and made them automatic.

4 - Transfer:

I transferred previous acquisitions several times during the process of learning to windsurf, in particular some which I learned in sailing.

I think I transferred part of this learning experience (fine sensitivities in my feet in particular) when I took up snow surfing.

## Learning to fly-fish

Pierre George, Besançon

When I took up fly-fishing, every time I went to the river, I only saw the trout when they fled. This produced two awarenesses in me: * I didn't know how to see the fish when they didn't move, and * they had seen me.

Long sessions of observation from the top of a bridge, careful not to move, allowed me to become aware * of the incredible way trout can blend into their surroundings. Standing there, looking down, I learned to see the fish. To begin with, I only noticed those which moved to take food. Then, noticing where they had moved from and where they went to, * I became aware of the places they stay in: any obstacle forming a counter-current, an eddy, where * they can remain without an effort. Thus, knowing where to look, I discovered them little by little. Another day, squatting behind a tree, I watched two trout swimming slowly in deep water. Two hikers went by about ten meters away. * They were not visible to the trout, as a screen of vegetation hid them. Seeing the trout flee as fast as they could, * I became aware that day of the faculty fish have of detecting vibrations produced by our steps on the river bank.

Another aspect of simply learning to approach and see the fish is the sun, which poses several problems.

When I began trout fishing, I immediately became aware that * if I was standing on a river bank looking into the sun, the surface of the water shone like a mirror and * I couldn't see anything taking place below the surface. Spontaneously, I put my hand to my eyes to shade them and * noticed a slight decrease in the amount of reflection. Putting on a hat or a cap, * it was easier to see and * my hands were free to fish. But the real revelation for me was the discovery of polarised glasses. One day, I was looking into the sun, trying to scrutinise the shining surface of the mirror before me, when a friendly fisherman gave me his glasses to try. I was dumbfounded: * the surface of the water became transparent. I * became aware that the problem of reflections and glare only concerns the fisherman, and not the fish. I was able to see with the glasses that the fish could see me perfectly clearly. Since that day, polarised glasses have become an accessory I can no longer do without when I'm trout fishing at the edge of the water.

Now that I was mastering the problems of getting close to the fish, I * became aware that the sun made things even more difficult if it was behind me. * The slightest shadow projected into the field of vision of a fish, even the tip of the rod, alerts it. Having alerted many fish in my fruitless attempts to get closer, but having always noticed <u>where</u> they hid, I * became aware later that the further a fish is from his hide-out, the more he is wary and vigilant.

I also noticed that * when insects hatch all at once, or * when minnows group together to spawn, the feeding activity of the fish, prudent to begin with, becomes less and less so. In these cases, a fish, * very present to his activity, can * more easily be approached and enticed. On the other hand, a wary fish swimming away as fast as it can * makes the others wary, and can even make one or more others take flight. In small streams particularly, a person who walks carelessly can * trigger off a chain reaction over several hundred metres.

Having learned to get near the fish, the fisherman can hope to catch some. From season to season, he will become aware that * stormy days on which the barometer falls suddenly are good days for fishing. He will also know, if he has caught fish and if they have stayed in his basket, that * in stormy weather, the flesh of a dead fish goes off more quickly. Having become aware that * the innards are what goes off fastest, because they contain semi-digested food, he will have learned to clean his fish before he puts them away in his basket.

Autopsies of his victims will have taught him * the incredible diversity of food that trout eat: from * the smallest gnat to * the musk rat, without forgetting * mice, * frogs, * bees and * ants.

By this time, many years have passed since his first awarenesses as a future fly fisherman: * circles on the water are a trout eating. Knowing now how to catch fish, he will have become aware that * a fish which gulps with a splash is small. Big fish, when they eat, * produce a much more discrete gulp with less noise. He will know that * close to open beaches too, fish that gulp are usually small and not very wary, * that bigger trout can usually be found in rocky, wooded streams.

Having fished frantically without catching anything on an evening when the river literally boils with trout crazily eating insects as they hatch in large numbers, he will have become aware - an awareness of fundamental importance - that when insects hatch in great numbers, * trout eat in one spot, * with an absolutely regular rhythm. This discovery explains the failure to catch fish on previous occasions when they seemed to be an extremely easy prey, and, properly used, will allow spectacularly successful catches.

Another day, the surprise attack of a fish on the fly I was pulling from the water yielded the revelation that * moving the fly on the water can trigger the attack of the fish.

Thus, from season to season, from failure to success, each day's fishing is a new step in a permanent learning process.

Each aspect of fly-fishing that Pierre George describes could have become the object of a text at least as long as this one, if it had been described in detail. Each could have become the object of a description within the framework of the four stages of learning. Clearly, a complete description of fly-fishing would take hundreds of pages.

## Learning manual activities

The first two accounts in this section deal with learning artistic activities. Neither of the writers attempts to describe her activity from beginning to end, from stage 1 to stage 4. Both have concentrated their efforts on very tiny awarenesses, describing minute movements of their awareness as they came to grips with the techniques they have chosen to describe. This may well be because artistic activities do not lend themselves to rapid mastery.

In the first account, which is in two parts, Anne Laurent describes how she began learning to use a Chinese inkbrush. She begins by describing how she explored its use, using the feedback from what she saw and felt to modify what she did with it. She speaks of her awarenesses of the tiniest changes in the different variables: the pressure she applies, the quantity of ink she uses, the area covered by each movement of her arm...

In the second part of her description, Anne speaks more generally about what being aware of her awareness brings her in the process of learning.

In the second account, Christiane Rozet gives us a simple list of a series of awarenesses she had during a pottery course. This list gives us those of her awarenesses which she chose to express but it is clear from these that she was aware of many, many other awarenesses which must have taken place during the work. To write them all down would have been impossible.

The effect of these two accounts is quite different, but any student of awareness knows that both writers were aware of their awarenesses constantly at least for the time they describe here. This was the aim of the exercise.

## Learning to use a Chinese inkbrush

Anne Laurent, Geneva

There are books which explain and show how to use a Chinese inkbrush. From them, we get a theoretical idea of this technique. But as soon as one puts a Chinese inkbrush to paper, * one realises that theory has nothing to do with practice.

The first thing I learned was that * the muscular energy I need to use to put the brush in contact with the paper is different from the energy I use with an ordinary brush, which I can use quite well.

* The resistance of the bristles to the paper is different, * as is the ink, which does not adhere to the paper in the same way as paint does, and * which allows one to cover larger surfaces with one stroke of the brush. I had something new to learn.

I drew strokes, lines, curves and blotches... * My eyes informed me that I was pressing too hard or not hard enough. Seeing the first results, * I could, by an act of will, command my muscles to exert more or less pressure on the bristles. My perception told me, as a result of strokes which were too fine, that * I had to position the bristles perpendicular to the handle and push regularly and rapidly towards the edge. Thus there was a constant to and fro between an action which I voluntarily modified, the result produced, the feedback through my eyes and a new action which modified the muscular energy engaged in my fingers, my wrist and my forearm.

Little by little, my mastery of the instrument has grown and I am now certain of producing more satisfactory results.

Here is my commentary on my learning.

Since my childhood, I have become more and more aware.

Over the last few months, I have been aware of my awarenesses.

Since a few weeks ago, I think I know what it is to become aware.

Over the last few hours, I think I have learned what use there is in becoming more aware during the learning process. Awarenesses seem to me to be stages in this process.

As long as I have not become aware of the fact that the muscular energy I engage in my fingers and my arm during the process of learning to paint with a Chinese inkbrush is the direct consequence of what happens on the paper, I cannot make progress (in this precise learning process).

As soon as I become aware of the relationship between the energy involved and the result, I know that my problem is there and not in the colour of the ink I'm using, for example.

I then know immediately where to be present, where to put my awareness.

But the fact of becoming aware of something (as in this example) does not mean that the problem has been solved, only that I know exactly what to work on. From then on, I may need 10 hours, 100 hours, 1000 hours to arrive at a result which satisfies me, but I can make progress.

### Learning to throw a pot

Christiane Rozet, Besançon

I had been wanting to learn to throw pots for many years and I finally had the opportunity of getting into this activity quite recently. While I was enjoying manipulating the clay, I took the time to note down some of the awarenesses I had while I was working. Here they are, in chronological order.

* This stoneware clay is grey, very different from the red or white clays I was used to working with as a kindergarten teacher.

* This clay is prepared using very precise gestures that I don't know. It is not enough to simply hit the clay as I used to do with ordinary clays.

* This preparation requires a considerable physical effort from the beginner that I am.

* When I watch the teacher doing a demonstration throw and I listen to his explanations, I am aware that there are a huge number of important details to remember.

* During my first trial throw on the wheel, I become aware that I have to keep my two hands in contact with each other while I work. As soon as my hands stop touching each other, a fault appears in what I am throwing.

* My first block of clay is just about centred! That's sheer luck; my psyche has not yet had the time to come into operation!

* To 'raise' the clay and 'lower' it again in order to centre it, I use a certain amount of energy which seems to me to be much more than the teacher used for the same job.

* I become aware that I don't know how to take the finished piece off the wheel. I have to ask for help.

* I become aware during the day that a round mass of clay is easier to centre than a heap of clay in any old shape.

* I have to be very careful preparing the clay: a little bubble of air left in it leads to the piece being deformed; a small stone can have the same effect.

* It is easier for me to get the wheel moving with my feet and then put them on the footrest while my hands work; this avoids jerking and bumping and I am more stable.

* Every few seconds, my hands no longer slide easily over the clay, which makes me aware that the clay has dried and I have to wet my hands again.

* A piece which begins well centred can be de-centred by an abrupt movement or a moment of irregular pressure with my fingers.

* If some pieces finish up non-symmetrical, that means that the mass of clay was not perfectly centred.

* It is more difficult for me to throw a form with a flared mouth than a cylinder or a sphere.

* It's not me, it's the clay which decides what form it will take as it rises!

* I still don't have criteria to know how thick the base of my vase is if I don't measure it.

* If I make a big effort to centre the clay, my hands rub on the moving table of the wheel and my skin gets burnt.

* When I 'lower' the clay after having 'raised' it, I become aware that a small point forms in the exact centre of the surface and I can use this as a guide.

* When I move on to an electric wheel, the speed is not a problem, quite the contrary.

* All the pieces thrown by the beginners are of roughly the same shape.

* We can never manage to 'raise' a piece very high because we usually leave small air bubbles when we are preparing the clay and also because we don't centre it perfectly; and even if the piece was correctly centred to begin with, it is difficult not to de-centre it while we are working. Our gestures are not precise enough.

* If the bottoms of my pieces are thicker in the middle, this is because I increase the pressure when I get to the edge.

* When the clay reaches the limit of its plasticity, the piece inevitably collapses.

* When a bump appears on the side of a piece, I become aware that I don't know how to make it disappear.

* When I have trouble centring, I have to scrape the clay spread around the main mass. This scrapes my hands and causes jolting.

* If I clean up this clay spread around the table of the wheel as soon as I have centred my mass, the rest of the work is much easier.

* When I look at the pots made on the first day, I am aware of their faults and also of the progress I have made in three days.

* Although I am left-handed for many, many activities, it is easier for me to hollow out the clay with my right thumb.

* If I put my elbows on my knees and work on a little electric wheel, I have a more stable basis than if I work on a big wheel, either foot or electric.

* At the end of three days, I use less energy to centre my piece; I am less tense and my hands rub less on the table. (What a relief!)

* I am now able to use the pallet to create little marks on my pieces: I become aware that I have acquired stability and also confidence in the precision of my gestures.

* My gestures are becoming more and more precise, less abrupt; so a mass which starts off well-centred remains so during the whole job.

* For the final detailed finishing on the table of the wheel, the tools must be held firmly and at a certain angle.

* While I'm working on the final details, I become aware that I have become more precise. I am more stable than I was on the first day and my touch is more delicate because of the way my hands - my thumbs - come together.

* While I'm smoothing the finished piece with a wet sponge, I can feel under my fingers small imperfections that I didn't see.

* After having worked on the final details for the greater part of the day, I find it difficult to centre my clay.

* The black stone clay that the teacher gives us next is much less abrasive, much more pleasant to work with, but it stains our hands black.

* I've thrown about thirty pieces in five days and I can see evident progress between the first pieces and the last ones.

* After 4 p.m. on the last day, there are only three students left in the workshop, and the teacher, who has to leave us for a while, suggests that we do whatever we like. However, since it is too late for our pieces to be completely finished, they will probably be destroyed.

* I don't feel the need to succeed and manage to throw two candlesticks which I had not been able to do the previous day, because I was competing with another student. (My psyche took over...)

* For the first time, I can decide what shape the piece I'm working on will be. It is not the clay that decides for me!

* I still don't have a way of completely closing a sphere.

These texts can also help us to understand the relationship which exists between a teacher and a learner in a field such as painting or potting. First it is obvious that, even if the learner has another person as a teacher, most of the time the teacher and the learner are actually the same person. The learner is the one who launches trials and the teacher is the one who comments on what can be seen as a result of these experiments, and suggests the modifications necessary for the next experiment. The learner painter or potter oscillates constantly between the two roles.

If someone learns an artistic skill with the help of a teacher, her role is to inform the learner of the type of inner dialogue the particular activity requires and to furnish situations in which this inner dialogue can take place. The teacher can also be aware of the role feedback is playing in her attempts to develop the sensitivities of the learner. No language exists for talking about the necessary awarenesses in greater detail than the descriptions Anne and Christiane have given here, and in fact none is necessary. The teacher need only use words such as 'more' or 'less', which indicate to the learner that changes are necessary, what should be worked on next and in which direction a parameter needs changing. Since both the learner and the teacher are human, and since both have already learnt so much in their lifetimes, both can relate to what is visible, the object which is being produced. The painter, since he is actually moving the brush, or the potter, since he is actually moulding the clay, develops an intimate knowledge of the muscular movements necessary to produce each stroke, each form.

When we are not holding the brush or raising the clay, we can only develop an inkling into the full exploration that is actually needed, although we can become aware of the nature of the inner dialogue we would have to develop if we were to do this ourselves. This would seem to be the main thing a learner can take from a teacher. The learner must go through the process in order to develop the skills. There can be no substitute for experience gained in the actual doing.

This way of knowing will be presented in Chapter 7 and is called 'acquaintance'.

### Learning to type
The two texts which now follow are about the same activity, learning to type. They illustrate the fact that the *process* of learning is the same for the two people, even if the contents of their awarenesses differ. Indeed, all learners can and do adopt a strategy that is specific to themselves. But the process itself can only take place in one way - by means of a series of awarenesses.

Christine Chauvin applies her skill in observing her awarenesses and gives a very detailed description of what the learning process was for her. We have included her text as an example of a more completely described learning process than others have given.

Alain L'Hôte comments on the fact that noting his awarenesses takes his presence away from learning to type, and so diminishes his capacity to learn. This is the case when one begins to create the new level of awareness that is necessary if one wishes to observe one's awarenesses.

Learning to type can be dull at times. Notice that these two people tried at all times to inject a challenge into what they were doing, by giving themselves rules, limits and constraints.

### Learning to type (on an old-fashioned typewriter)
Christine Chauvin, Semur en Auxois
September

* When the assignment is given, I am aware that this job bores me because none of the subjects proposed interests me.

* During the trip back from Besançon, I become aware that I am more and more motivated by the idea of learning to type. I remember that before the age of 20, I wanted to learn (one of my sisters was learning and had a machine) but since then, I haven't really felt like it much.

* While I am driving, I become aware that I am mobilizing myself for learning to type.

How can I find a typewriter?

What do I know about typing?

* I have not had much contact with people typing except for the secretaries at some of the places where I work, and the little contact I have had has been very occasional. I * become aware that I have a general idea of the gestures one uses to place the sheet of paper in the machine because I've seen it done: * you turn a wheel on the right at the end of a roller ( * it makes a noise), * you line up the top and bottom edges of the paper and * you turn the wheel in the other direction to begin at the top of the sheet.

* There is a horizontal bar at the bottom for the spaces between the words.

* The first line of the typewriter contains the keys AZERTUIYOP. (Once I actually get my typewriter, I become aware that * I was making several errors in the order of the letters: UIY instead of: YUI.)

* There is a key on the side one presses on to get capitals.

* In order to type, you use all the fingers of both hands (each key always being moved by the same finger). You shouldn't look at the keyboard. These are the challenges I give myself.

* As soon as I get home, I become aware that I am ready to set about finding myself a typewriter. My first try gets nowhere. I contact another person and go and get the machine. I begin learning that same evening.

* First awareness: the typewriter has never been used and there is a whole series of blockages.

* Second awareness: I am disappointed. I expected to begin typing immediately. I am caught between the desire to begin learning and the irritation of having to waste time finding out what is blocking the mechanism.

* After a while, I get it working. I begin typing. * Awareness: very quickly, I have cramps in my arm and my shoulder, especially on the right-hand side. I push the typewriter a little further away on the table to have a comfortable position with my forearms resting on the table.

* I explore the first line of letters and * become aware that it is not quite as I thought it was. (See above.)

I * become aware that the line contains ten keys and that if I do not use my thumbs I only have eight fingers I can use. I make the hypothesis that the two index fingers look after two keys on this line. (* I am aware that I will have to ask someone.)

Sunday evening 24/9

I begin work on the top line. * Awareness: it is important to make the little fingers work; I use A and P (in small letters) then I add my index fingers; I make words (French or invented), with A R T Y U P with spaces between them. (Use of the right thumb.)

Monday evening 25/9

* I work with the same letters again, but I place my eight fingers (but not my thumbs) on the line below. I asked, and someone told me that the middle line is used as the base line for the fingers. * Awareness: I have to change what I learnt yesterday.

I * become aware that I have cramps again; I have to push the machine away from me and rest my forearms on the table. * Awareness: I didn't use yesterday's experience straightaway to place the machine in the right spot.

To begin with, I use the letters two by two to make sequences of two repeated letters as an exercise, but I * become aware that I want to make words with spaces, with my eyes closed. Writing words attracts me more.

I * become aware that I have not mastered the use of the roller. * I have noticed which button allows one to keep the sheet of paper squeezed round the roller but I don't know which position of the button holds the paper in place.

Tuesday 26/9

I * become aware that I still have problems with this same button blocking or unblocking the paper.

Thursday 28/9

For the first time I am going to continue typing on a sheet of paper I have already begun to use; I * become aware that I have to introduce the paper into the machine a certain way: the sheet has to be presented upside down with the side I don't want to write on facing me.

I * become aware that I still don't rest my forearms spontaneously; I tire quickly.

I * become aware that I still hesitate when I'm using the button which locks the sheet of paper round the roller.

I * become aware that I still have to work on the same letters; I don't make many mistakes but I go slowly.

I * become aware that I am at the end of a line but that the word is not yet finished. Where is the dash which will allow me to cut the word? I try the one on key 6, * it works. I * become aware that the dash on key 6 is half way up the letter, whilst * the dash on key 8 is under the other letters: I can use this one for underlining and the one on key 6 for crossing out a word.

I * become aware that I make mistakes sometimes between P and A when I am typing, although at the beginning I knew which was on the right and which was on the left, because I knew the line A Z E R T ... O P.

I * become aware that I can do another interesting thing by exploring the stock of French words I can type with these few letters at my disposal. I * become aware that this challenge makes my learning more attractive.

I * become aware after a time that while I was looking for words, I had forgotten that U was one of the letters that I knew.

While typing the word "râpa", I * become aware that I don't have the circumflex accent. I * become aware that I can add this new key within the restrictions I have given myself, because of its place on the keyboard.

I need capitals. I * become aware that I can also add this key which is close to those I know.

* A short time after having stopped typing, while I am occupied with other activities, I become aware that other words are coming to me which I could write. Consequently, I * become aware that I am still with the preceding exercise.

I type some more this same day: I * become aware then that if I type the circumflex accent before the letter which needs it, I won't have to backspace one after I've typed it.

Friday 29/9

I add one key: E. I write on a sheet of paper placed to the right of the machine all the keys I have at my disposal: Capitals, A E R T Y U P

I * become aware that when I look at this sheet to try to find words and sentences in French, it is easier to type: I work better with my fingers when I am looking at something.

Saturday 30/9

I * become aware that my errors are due either to hitting the wrong one of two keys side by side or to typing with a right finger what should have been typed with the equivalent left finger. (I type P for A or the opposite.)

I * become aware that I can't yet manage to introduce the sheet into the typewriter the right way round first off. I hesitate, I put the sheet behind the slot where it should go. But once the sheet is in the machine, I know what to do, except that * I forget to check the position on the roller: the sheet is too far to the left or the right and I have to begin the whole operation of installing the paper again.

I * become aware that certain sequences of letters are pleasant to type; for example TRE, ERT or REZ.

As fatigue sets in, * I type two keys side by side at the same time more and more often, with the result that the arms get stuck near the sheet of paper.

I * become aware that I don't have any more problems with the left hand than with the right.

Sunday 1/10

I * become aware that, since I became aware the day before that I was forgetting to place the paper laterally using the markers on the bar, I don't make this mistake any more. I install the paper correctly straight away.

I * become aware that I have all the vowels of French except those which have grave or acute accents; * all the vowels are placed on the same line: A E Y U I O.

While I can now consider myself competent at a whole line, A Z E R T Y U I O P, as well as the keys for caps and the circumflex accent, I * become aware that I have no idea what letters are below the ones I know.

I add the key which is on the right hand end of the next line down, M, and, shortly after, the symmetrical key, Q. I * become aware that I can introduce them almost simultaneously.

I * become aware that several times, I miss the key Y (I type U instead) which is typed with the right hand, although I master the key T (which is symmetrical with it, typed with the left index finger).

Wednesday 4/10

I now add the letters S and L almost at the same time, exploring the line below the one I know from one key to its neighbour. This same day, for variety, I introduce a letter and some signs from the top line:

- the dash on key 6, typed in order to separate words or groups of words;
- the apostrophe;
- the letter à.

I * become aware of the fact that now that I have begun to explore and use this top line, the line I worked on to begin with, it seems much closer than before to the middle line on which I base my fingers.

I * become aware of the nature of the mistakes I make:

* There are mistakes of horizontal proximity:

> e → z ; a → z; t → r; m → ù or %; e → r

( * another awareness: the letters go towards the left as well as to the right)

* mistakes of vertical priority:

> a → q; p → m; 6 → t

* mistakes of symmetry (one hand types instead of the other, but with the same finger):

> e → i

* mistakes due to a bad position of the fingers to begin with. (The letters are shifted one key laterally):

poussette → pouddryyr (right hand badly placed)

reste → ezqrz (left hand badly placed)

Thursday 5/10

I add two keys from the top line: 'é' and 'ç'. * Typing the keys on this line is relatively difficult (an awareness). The mistakes are more frequent. * They are mistakes of horizontal proximity:

é → 3 or "

or, * even more often, * mistakes of vertical proximity:

é → z; 6 → y; 6 → t

I * become aware that, among the letters which I am still not using, I miss some more than others for making phrases and sentences. * 'n' is the one I miss most, since I can't make sentences with a plural subject; I don't have at my disposal certain endings in the conjugation: *ons, ent, ont, ant...*

Where I am at now, I * become aware that I can make long phrases using as many as possible of the keys I have. * I am aware of the attraction of a game which consists of making complex sentences with the restriction of a limited number of letters, but which, being an assembly of words chosen for their letters, often ends up with a surprising, surreal or amusing meaning... (e.g. *La toute petite portée pratiquée ça et là a été remarquée par l'armée alarmée mais pas alarmiste. Marie est pratique pour partir pour l'Amérique. Il se peut qu'Odette reste ailleurs qu'à Semur pour ses petits pieds d'oie. Le restaurateur adore les moules rôties au poulet pour le repas de sa petite Miquette adorée qui les papouille sur le dôme. Etc*).

Wednesday 11/10

In an old catalogue, I happen upon the typewriter I am using. I read the description to see if there is anything I haven't discovered by myself. I * become aware that the button which deals with the ribbon has three positions although the ribbon only has two colours; the third position is for stencils. I * become aware that I don't understand one of the sentences of the description: "compensated space bar allowing the insertion of a forgotten letter and the equalization of lines at the right of a text". * I am aware that I will have to ask someone if I want to find out how to use this feature. I read "three positions of type adjustment." I look for this, find it and study this adjustment.

Reading the description of the other typewriters on the page, I * become aware that not all have the same number of keys on the keyboard: the others have 44 keys (88 signs) and mine has only 43 (86 signs).

When I begin typing on Wednesday, 11th October, * I have the impression that I don't know anything anymore. It seems to me that I have no trace of my experience left in my fingers. After a few minutes, I * become aware that it comes back very quickly.

When I give myself the task of retyping a long sentence with the intention of not making a single mistake, I * become aware that I don't make the preceding mistakes (except some which are persistent), but that * I make others, where I had no problems before.

I * become aware that the letters on the middle line to the right are in alphabetical order: J K L M and are typed with the fingers of the same hand.

End of October

Continuing with this learning experience, I * become aware of the sequence of consonants: D F G H J K L M in alphabetical order (continuation of the preceding awareness).

After adding the N, I * become aware that I only have to learn the most unusual consonants of the French language: I * become aware that these consonants are all worth more than one point in the game of Scrabble.

## Learning to type

Alain L'Hôte, Besançon

This learning experience took place on a Macintosh using the software "Mac Tap".

The aim of the first exercise proposed by the software author is "to get the fingers moving easily and to learn the layout of the keyboard", using the right finger to type the key required on the screen. This is the only part of the exercise I will describe: because of the way the software is built, it can last for hours and is never really finished.

Lesson 0

Reading the manual for the software, I learn the first "simple but essential" rule: "Always keep your fingers on the home line. QSDF for the four fingers of the left hand, JKLM for the four fingers of the right hand, and the thumbs on the space bar."

Lesson 1

Starting with my fingers in the home position, I type the letters asked for on the screen, moving my fingers in a 'scientific' way. E.g., to go to such and such letter, I have to move my left hand middle finger one line higher and two spaces to the right. I * become aware of the inefficiency and the slowness of my method and also of the risk of error, the keys being very sensitive.

I change my strategy: * I will type by guesswork. Even if there are mistakes on the page, I imagine that this will get better with practice.

* It's difficult to bring my fingers back to the home line after having typed a character.

I stop typing: * it's time to eat and * my fingers are sore.

Lesson 2 (Typing by guesswork)

NB. The description of the following sessions were written at the same time as my learning experience was taking place, or, rather, parallel to it.

* If I use the finger indicated on the screen, I am almost certain I'll land on the right key. * There is a logic in the use of certain fingers.

* The right-hand middle finger is difficult to move alone.

* The keys situated at the extremities (£, 1, W, B, N, Y, *, etc...) are the most difficult to reach. In the near future, since I can do so with this software, I will select the fingers for these keys and make them work by themselves.

* The fingers of my left hand are less well-oriented than those of my right hand. This is surprising for a left-hander.

* The correct finger goes to the key required more 'instinctively'. * At this level, I am starting to master it. That gives me encouragement to go on.

* Good God! I have just discovered that keys D and K on my keyboard have a little bump on them. This will help me! These are the keys the middle fingers are supposed to be on. * Key 5 on the numerical keyboard also has a bump; that's news to me.

* When I anticipate what I am going to write for my learning diary while I am typing, I make lots more mistakes. Ah! Presence!

* I have too many ideas to be present with my work. I'm stopping for this evening.

Lesson 3

* It's so much fun typing that I forget to write my reflections on my learning. My fingers whizz and fly over the keyboard, which produces mistakes but also an agreeable tactile sensation and a feeling that what I am doing is right.

* My wrist is starting to hurt.

(Pause)

* I try to move the end fingers - those which correspond to the extremities of the keyboard - one key more than required. * It works.

Lesson 4

I * become aware that many errors come from the weight of the hand which is not typing and which presses involuntarily on the keys. I will have to try to be present in both hands at the same time.

* I try to make myself more sensitive to keys D and K (bumps - reference points), because I am aware that they really are the two pivots of the keyboard.

* More dexterity for all my fingers, coupled with the discovery of the keys D and K, allows me to look out for my middle fingers a little more carefully. A small improvement but it's still not very good!

CONCLUSION

* The role of my presence, of my capacity to concentrate on the job, is one of the important factors of the progress I have made.

* The role of successive awarenesses is obvious. Each time I changed something or modified my approach, an awareness was the reason behind it.

* The role of sensitivity is important. Twice, when I had the feeling I was making progress, I felt sure of myself and I worked with enthusiasm.

* Knowing by touching. This is something relatively new for me, but it has been very important.

* As soon as one area has been learnt, it allows me to concentrate on another problem.

* Bringing my fingers back to 'home position' has still not been really dealt with. * I realize that I didn't give it the priority I should have; but, one problem at a time, please.

## Learning experiences from everyday life

In this section, the two examples are taken from everyday lives. They could have been written by anybody who has learnt to be aware of the processes of learning - who, in more technical terms, has become aware of his awarenesses, at least partially. They describe simple acts of living and show how we adapt to the world as it presents itself to us moment by moment.

The examples involve discoveries which make the life of the person easier in some small way, but their importance for us lies in the banality of the field of experience they describe.

Marie-Thérèse Saint-Hillier wanted to make a hot drink for her mother on her mother's gas stove. She describes how she managed to get the stove working. This process reached stage three, but had not reached stage four at the time of writing. She still needs to think about what she is doing in order to avoid mistakes.

Fusako Allard learnt to close a metal screen in the building where she works. It took her about a week to automatise her movements and roll down the screen exactly right. It is easy to see the four stages of learning in her description.

These examples are designed to show, then, that to live is to become aware.

## Learning to use a gas stove

Marie-Thérèse Saint-Hillier, Besançon

A couple of days ago, I had to use a gas stove that was new to me.

My mother was ill and wanted a hot drink, so I went into her kitchen and after putting water in a saucepan without even thinking about it, I put out my left hand towards the second button and the right towards the spark button - a reflex because I do it so often in my own home! * Ah! Why the strange feeling? * Of course! I'm not at home, it's not my stove! I realised my mistake immediately. Anyhow, it's not a problem. I know how to use one gas stove and I can certainly use another one! I looked at the front of the stove... * Blast! It's too dark to read the buttons! I lean over and look for the spark button. * It's on the left, and not on the right as mine is. I straighten up and try to light the burner again. I press on the spark button on the left and the burner second from the right... * it still doesn't work. What's the problem? I think for a moment. * Ah yes! My mother always turns off the gas at the wall, whereas I don't. I open the tap at the wall and try again. * It works! ... but not really, * because it's not the right burner! So I also have to check the order of the burner knobs. * The first one on the right corresponds to the small burner; it's not the same as my stove. All right! I straighten up again and, carefully and with concentration, I press with my left hand on the spark button and with my right, I turn the first knob. This time, * it works. My mother will get her drink.

For several days, I systematically made the same mistakes and had to think about what I had to do. Each time, the awarenesses came more and more quickly. However, every time I didn't think about it, I made the same mistakes.

## Learning to close a metal screen

Fusako Allard, Osaka

On the second floor of the building where I work, there is a metal screen which has to be rolled down and locked by the last person leaving that floor of the building. When I moved in, I arranged with the caretaker that he would roll it down to where I could reach it and that I would lock it every evening when I left work.

The first evening, I pulled on the screen so hard that * it rolled right down to the floor and * bounced back up out of my reach. It was terrible. I couldn't reach it, so I couldn't close it. The second night, I was much more careful. * I rolled it down, * pressing gradually on it, testing how much energy I should put in my arms to pull it down and then I pulled it down all the way and that was fine. But then I wanted to do it faster, so I had to learn what was the fastest without it bouncing back again, making a terrible sound.

I did it many times and I finally got to the point where I was pulling down and I didn't have to do anything. Now it just goes down to the floor and all I have to do is lock it. Now I don't think about it anymore. It is completely automatic. I just pull it and lock it. I can be talking to a friend or thinking about something else.

It took me about a week to learn exactly how much energy to use to roll the screen down so that it would just reach the floor.

## Learning in fewer than four stages

Many examples of learning can also be found in which, for some reason, not all four stages are present. Sometimes, only stage one can be seen or only stages one and two can be expected to exist. Similarly, some learning requires only an initial awareness and mastery is immediate, since the process itself is already known.

Fusako Allard gives us an example of a learning process which took place in one single awareness. It involves using an escalator in Kobe. No further learning is required once the essential awareness has taken place.

## Taking an escalator

Fusako Allard - Osaka

There is an escalator in a station in Kobe. The minute you are on the first step, it starts moving. I got to the monorail station and I thought it wasn't operating, so I was climbing the stairs and I looked and saw this man going up. I thought: "My goodness! The operator didn't do this for me but did it for this man". The next time I was there, it wasn't operating, so I said: "Would you put this on so I can ride it?" He said: "It's automatic. All you have to do is walk towards it and it will begin working."

## Learning to change oneself

This chapter ends with two accounts provided by people who deliberately set out to modify long-standing behaviours in order to live their lives differently.

Usually, the behaviours we give ourselves during our lives function perfectly well automatically. As the word indicates, the main characteristic of an automatism is that it functions best when we don't think about it, that is to say, it requires no presence. We constantly make gestures and movements without being present to what we are doing, and this is as it should be. At most, we may become aware that the gesture has just been made by itself, as it were.

In order to change a behaviour, we have to manage to be present systematically each time it takes place so as to be able to intervene and undo the automatism which drives it and which may have been functioning for years without our presence. It is easy to see why it can be so difficult to change an automatism.

Foreign language behaviour can become fossilised very easily, especially when it is the result of automatisms carried over from the mother tongue. The teacher's role in such a case - whether the teacher and the learner are one and the same person or not - is to work on the learner's presence, rather than on the content.

The first account describes the way in which a young Muslim woman learns to go into a café in France and drink a glass of beer. She allows us to get a glimpse of the fears she experiences when she does this for the first time. Many people will be able to recognise aspects of themselves in this description, even if they have never had the same experience.

The second example tells of the way in which Alain L'Hôte who had smoked for twenty years learns to become a non-smoker.

## Going into a café in France

Author anonymous, Besançon

When I arrived in France five years ago now, all I knew about the country were the images I had collected from reading or from listening to people who had lived here. So I had everything to learn about the French way of life.

For example, * I had noticed that many people, especially young people, went to cafés, and this was an important awareness. In my country, very few men or women would go into a café, as life is very different from in France, so I had never been in a café in my life. It was an unknown world that I wanted to discover, since it seemed interesting to know about a place which attracted so many people and which belonged to the habits of the country. So * I became aware of the attraction cafés had for me, of my curiosity about this so typical French place. Invited by a French friend, I finally decided to "go and have a drink", as they say, at the Café du Théâtre.

But * I became aware that I was a little frightened to go into this place which was so unusual for me; two girls going into a public place alone - a place which served alcohol as well - it seemed unreal to me, and so far from my habits! I told myself I had to go beyond my fears which, * I was aware, came from the education I had received which forbade me to go into such places.

As I walked through the door of the Café du Théâtre, I was very uneasy, and * I was very aware of this feeling of embarrassment because I could feel my heart beating faster. I had the impression everyone was looking at us - and especially me! I said this to my friend who told me to look and check if it were the case. I looked furtively at the other people and * realised that no one was bothering about us. Ouf! We had made it in unnoticed! When the moment came to order, my friend ordered a beer, and I expected the waiter to refuse to bring it to her. To my surprise, * I realised, watching his reactions, that he wasn't even surprised.

"So", I said to myself, "in France, a girl can drink whatever she wants to, even alcohol." Watching the other people, * I saw that some girls had alcoholic drinks in front of them. I decided to order one too... and was amazed when the waiter served me without any difficulty. * So I became aware that in France, I too was free to drink what I liked. And I also became aware that * this was me, a Muslim girl stamped with a certain education, who had ordered a beer and that * I was drinking something forbidden in my country! Pushed by curiosity and the example the other girls gave me, I had surmounted my apprehension and * I saw that my discovery of this new world was not in fact so difficult or terrifying. Later, I even suggested to friends that we go to a café and "have a drink" and * I saw that going into a café was not unusual for a girl.

So my embarrassment disappeared and I knew from my experience that I was not the target of everyone's scorn.

I can now order a beer knowing that the waiter will not look askance at me. I now feel at ease in cafés and have lost my fear of "not being in my place"... * I have also become aware that repeating a certain situation helps to drain away one's fears. I can now go into any café I like, and not limit myself to the Café du Théâtre. By learning that going into a café was not forbidden, I learnt that I could do it without feeling ill-at-ease or embarrassed.

* And I learnt that other places are also open to me, such as a billiard room where I go from time to time.

But from this experience, * I became aware, too, of the diversity of ways of living which can exist in two different cultures, and I am less surprised by certain things French people do which seemed so strange and so different from my earlier life. In the end, * I have realised that life is short and that we can all profit from it, everyone according to his taste.

### Learning to stop smoking

Alain L'Hôte - Besançon

This was not an idea which came to me suddenly. It's been on my mind for more than a year.

Sunday 1/10 at the end of the afternoon:

* I know what I'm going to work on: I'm going to learn not to smoke.

Monday 2/10 all day:

1. * I am aware that throwing out my packet of tobacco - I roll my own - is difficult, and I put off the moment of actually doing it.

2. * I become aware that I have to fix myself an S-Day, when I will stop. So this Friday at midnight, I will STOP. That leaves me with another two packets to burn ...!

Same day, in the evening:

1. * I become aware that it is a good thing to have given myself a 'respite' of four days: this way, I give myself the time to think about my decision and to observe the smoker in me.

2. * I decide to cut out the 'superfluous cigarettes': the ones I smoke through habit and not because I feel like them.

Tuesday 3/10:

* I become aware in two stages of the lack of precision of the challenge I gave myself on Sunday. It has to be more precise. I will:

- learn not to smoke finally and permanently,
- learn not to smoke finally and permanently without medical help (chemistry, acupuncture or other ways...)

4.45 pm, coming out of school:

1. * I become aware that I have just lit up a 'superfluous cigarette': I can't get rid of them.

2. * I become aware that it is more and more difficult for me to make the distinction between the ones I am smoking from habit and the ones I feel like smoking: they have all become indispensable.

3. * I become aware that this doesn't worry me: it doesn't put the rest of my experiment in danger.

5.15 pm:

Although I don't feel like smoking, * I become aware that I can taste in my mouth the same thing as a few years ago (when I tried to give up smoking another time). I re-live the same state, difficult to describe.

5.30 pm:

1. * Well! I feel like a smoke! I light up.

2. * I become aware that I like to have a cigarette in my mouth: the smoke deliciously tickles the inside of my nostrils! It's so good!

3. * I decide not to keep the cigarette in my mouth.

4. * I catch myself red-handed at least ten times. Each time, I quickly put the cigarette down on the ashtray.

5. * I become aware that I don't get as much pleasure smoking if I put the cigarette down between each puff.

5.50 pm:

I put out the cigarette regretfully. Home-made cigarettes are smoked slowly, and they burn themselves out slowly too.

1. * The strange sensation in my mouth comes back.

2. My wife comes home from work. * I become aware that the sensation disappears.

All that, my dear friend, takes place in the psyche. Do you know how one gets into the psyche?

7 pm:

Another cigarette is in the ashtray and smoking. * I become aware that I also like to breathe the smell. This is new for me, and * makes me aware that I do not really know myself as a smoker.

Wednesday 3/10:

1. * I become aware that I like to pass my lower lip over my moustache: I like the 'taste' of cigarettes.

2. * I have a lot of trouble not keeping my cigarette in my mouth. Often I keep it in my mouth while I'm doing something where my two hands are occupied.

3. * I'm in front of the computer. My eyes are fixed on a ball of ash which has been on the desk for days: today it irritates me.

4. * I become aware that I have to get rid of the cigarette environment. * My morning coffee gives me the urge to smoke: tomorrow, I'll drink tea.

5. * My packet of tobacco will soon be finished. I can still buy another one – 40 grams for two days. In fact, I will buy a packet of ready rolled Gauloises: I know I don't like them much. This will be a way of edging away from roll-your-own tobacco that I like so much.

6. * It seems to me that I have smoked less today, but I have no way of knowing for sure. * I am aware that I have been thinking about my challenge all day and that certain cigarettes were less interesting than others.

Thursday 4/10:

From today, I only smoke ready-rolled Gauloises.

6.45 am to 7.00 am (driving to school):

1. * This is my first ready-made Gauloise of the morning, the first I've smoked for many years. As I expected, after a cup of tea, it's not much good.

2. * I find the first puff terribly strong, my tongue stings, it's all furry.

3. * At a bus stop, a man is lighting up a cigarette. I am surprised to find his gesture ridiculous.

4. * I become aware that I have to be wary of such a reaction. (I remember having had the same experience the first time I tried to stop smoking.) In other words, I have to keep working on myself without thinking I've won.

5. * I become aware that I notice everybody who lights a cigarette.

At morning study (after 7.20 am):

I stopped correcting my pupils' exercise books in order to write what follows.

1. * I put my presence in my mouth and I feel like a cigarette. A child comes into the room: "Hello!" ... and I forget what is happening in my mouth.

2. * I don't have the same criteria for saying that a cigarette is 'superfluous': I don't really feel like smoking, but some puffs seem to me to be marvellous.

11.30 am:

I give myself the challenge of not smoking the ritual cigarette in the car between school and the house.

Midday:

 * I become aware that I want to begin eating as fast as possible so I won't feel like smoking: * the cigarette just before the meal is the one I miss most.

12.40 pm:

My wife has to go to work. I'm going to sleep for 45 minutes. * It's not just by chance that I feel sleepy.

5.30 pm:

* Each time I do something manual, I feel like smoking. This time is no exception.

Friday 6/10 (S Day):

I woke up in the middle of the night and one word came into my mind: "smoke" ... and I went back to sleep. * It's getting worked on in my sleep!

Before 10.00 am:

* Every cigarette seems to be 'superfluous'.

10.00 am, the break:

 * I feel like smoking; I feel it in my stomach; I'm hungry.

11.30 am, the end of the morning's class:

* I'm very hungry, my stomach is "crying out". Although I had decided not to smoke between 11.30 and midday, * I find myself with a cigarette in my mouth. * I become aware that * my hunger has disappeared, and that * I took out this cigarette and lit it unconsciously.

Between 12.00 and 1.30 pm:

1. My wife is not coming home for lunch today, and I get back into my old bachelor's habits. * These habits trigger in me a very strong desire to smoke.

2. * I smoke the last cigarette in the packet: the 20 grams have lasted one and a half days. I've 'won' a half a day, although I was not really aiming to do so.

3. * To celebrate the last cigarette this evening, with the last puff, I'm going to switch on the smoke detector.

In the evening:

1. * I become aware that, as the fateful hour comes closer,

* I'm not smoking as much as I would like to, I'm holding back;

* I feel like giving up this challenge I've given myself;

* To hold on, I reason with myself, finding a pile of good reasons not to give in.

* As I write this, I feel a pressure on my temples.

Sunday 8/10, in the evening:

I haven't taken any notes since I gave up smoking. Here is what I remember.

1. * Today at the end of the day, I had a difficult time. I slept to chase away my 'bad thoughts'.

 2. * Generally speaking - apart from what I have just written - I am not finding this too difficult to put up with.

 3. * There are very specific moments during which I feel like smoking:

> * at the end of a job, when I unwind;

> * at the end of this weekend, during which I did so much.

4.       I've taken to chewing bits of liquorice wood: * I catch myself holding them like a cigarette, * drawing on them, * throwing them away like a butt when they get too short.

Monday 9/10:

Concerning point 3 from Sunday - I thought I had my ideas straight on the subject. In fact, I feel things very clearly, but it is very difficult to express them because everything is so subtle:

1. * It seems obvious to me that every time I feel like smoking, there is a trigger behind it.

2. * And it's the trigger that's difficult to talk about: smelling someone else's cigarette isn't a trigger, but anticipating that I will stay back in my classroom for 5 minutes after class - a thing I rarely do - is.

3. * I feel very 'Pavlov's dog'. It's the evocation of a situation - or a series of situations - which triggers my desires to smoke.

4. * These evocations are furtive and very diverse.

Note: If you see Gattegno in the corridor, you can tell him that it's true that evocation is really one of our powers, and it works very well, a bit too well even!!!

Other remarks: * I become aware that I have reflected at length for several days in order to make some stupid discoveries:

1. * Smoking is learnt.

2. * When it's learnt, like everything else that's learnt, it becomes automatic.

3. And when something is automatic, in what drawer is it kept? ...

4. * At the least stimulus, the automatism responds marvellously well.

5. * When I decided to stop smoking, I wondered what part my soma had in this habit. Now I know that the answer to that will help me solve my problem as I want to solve it, which is definitively and with the powers I can find within myself.

6. * I don't see very clearly how I can work on my psyche: the best thing is not to reply to its demands.

7. * Eating liquorice wood has been a great help to me, but I don't want to become dependent upon it. I am going to use it as little as possible.

Tuesday 10/10:

1. Considering where I am at already, I can't really allow myself to put on weight. * But I am eating more and more.

 2. * After four days without smoking, the car still smells of stale tobacco.

3. * Before Saturday, I had never smelt the smell of stale tobacco in the car, and I wondered why in the classified ads people take the trouble to say that the owner is a non-smoker!

 * Now I can smell the same smell in the den.

Wednesday 10th and the following days:

In fact, there is nothing more to add. From day to day, things are the same and I have to struggle. Often I say to myself: "Why give up something so good?"

However, I do have a few modifications:

1. I gave up liquorice wood for cloves: * liquorice was irritating for my tongue and made me think about cigarettes too much.

2. I stopped drinking aperitifs because * they triggered the desire to smoke.

I weighed myself to see if stopping smoking would lead to me putting on weight.

June, two years later:

Here is the state of affairs after a year and eight months.

1. I put on weight - 12 kilos. Now I have to learn to eat correctly. What a life!

2. My wife tells me I wasn't particularly pleasant for several months.

3. My desire to smoke has almost completely disappeared now, but it is as if I kept it alive in order to remain vigilant:

* I often talked about what I did.

* I often said to myself: "In these circumstances, I would have smoked."

4. The smokers around me don't put me out, except when they don't smoke:

* they often have bad breath.

* their clothes often smell strongly of stale tobacco.

5. I feel anger towards the people who write ads about giving up smoking. They are liars:

* No, I don't feel better now than before. * My joints hurt, * my stomach hurts...

6. * I have the impression that the smoke wants to get out of me: blotches, pimples and bumps of all kinds have appeared on my skin.

7. I have the impression of a new force in me: now * I know I can undertake any change.

# 7  On knowing

Gattegno pointed out that there is a considerable range of phenomena covered by the word 'knowledge':

> In my pocket diary there are a few pages devoted to holding names, addresses and telephone numbers of a number of people and institutions with which I have some dealings. The fact that I carry these sheets around, tells me:
>
> a.  that I must know they exist and why,
>
> b.  that I must know how to use the list,
>
> c.  that when I look at any one of the entries I can associate with the name either a blank or an image or some excitement, dismay or any one of several feelings, proving that I can be triggered by the impact, first upon my eyes and brain and then my consciousness, of those signs on paper,
>
> d.  that I know which marks refer to a person, which to a location and which to whether I am far or near from that place, whether I am in possession of enough means to call from a pay phone ... .
>
> ... In fact I am faced at once with the difference between knowledge that is memorized, knowledge that results from impacts, knowledge that is association, knowledge that is images, knowledge of doubt or certainty, knowledge as awareness, knowledge as skills and knowledge of knowledge, etc. (1976 V 5:2)

If the awareness is the basic unit of learning (see Chapter 5) and knowledge is a result of learning, we can immediately ask what relationship there is between awareness and knowledge. Gattegno described various aspects of this in the same newsletter (p.4):

- Awareness is wider than knowledge. Awareness can vanish without leaving a trace but if it does leave one then there is the
  possibility for knowledge to exist as a result.
- Awareness is the way that a knower holds the thing to be known
  so that it can make its impact.
- The mind uses awareness to scan the field to be known.
- Awareness is needed to work on knowledge again if knowledge
  must be changed, made more conscious, more precise, more con-
  nected, and so on.

Thus awareness creates knowledge and awareness acts on knowledge. But
the self knows that the creation and the action are not the same as the
knowledge itself, the content of the awareness. They are both part of the
process of knowing which leaves knowledge behind after energy and time
have been spent producing or manipulating it.

'Knowing' is therefore a process which is at the heart of all learning.

Clearly the exploration and practice that form stages two and three of the
learning process are aspects of knowing. Clearly, too, awareness is central
in knowing, and knowledge (and know-hows) can be seen as energy that
has been structured by a process of knowing.

What activities does knowing encompass? Among others, Gattegno described the following:

- Knowing determines what we need to acquire now and what we
  can postpone.
- Knowing makes us pay attention to natural hierarchies in the
  field.
- Knowing leads us to be concerned with retention,
- ... with testing,
- ... with considering what has to be done.

Knowing, then, is the activity of the mind that sorts out the many demands of learning complex activities.

When one recognises knowing as it takes place in oneself, one knows firstly that either knowledge or know-hows are being generated from it, and
secondly that one is changing oneself for the future, not just adding something to one's memory.

It is the dynamics of knowing which produces either knowledge or
know-hows, available and usable in living one's life. But the person
who has a know-how available is not the same person who did not

have it available before learning it. To learn is not to accumulate knowledge, but to change oneself. Thus knowledge is a by-product of acts of learning which have been lived. (1979 IX 2:7)

When we become a painter, a sportsperson or a mathematician, what do we do? Certainly we accumulate knowledge about the field, but this is not the essential thing. The development we need comes about through applying the process of knowing repeatedly in the field in question; this is what changes us, and knowing is therefore what we cultivate in ourselves. Knowledge arrives as a by-product, generated automatically and retained.

With this understanding, teaching can be recast not as a means to transmit knowledge, but as the way to encourage the right kinds of knowing, from which the knowledge that is desired will emerge.

Here are some examples of exercises which do this; which encourage the right kinds of knowing.

### Knowing as a painter knows
How does someone learn to be a painter?

> In 1957 I was in Addis Ababa. I had a mission with the United Nations to work on science books for secondary schools – that was the assignment – but I had diplomatic status, because the UN sent me there, so I was in contact with people who were in the other diplomatic circles, and I asked them if they wanted to form a club, a painting club. They agreed, and they came. I became a teacher of painting. I would have shown you here if we had done this, how, having worked on myself in order to shake away the two mistakes I had made so far ['anybody can be creative but me' and that others were the judge of whether or not I was creative], I could produce things; whether they were of value or no value is an additional component. I didn't want to be concerned with that; I was concerned with the act itself. I taught these people in Addis Ababa to paint. And I'll tell you how. You can do it at home. The first thing I did was to say, "Never do any work on a white or one-coloured surface. Take two pages of a newspaper and put them on the wall. The newspaper is full of print – all sorts of things – advertisements, writing, bold characters, ..."

We had paint and wash because it's the one that I learnt with first, so I passed it on to others, and I told them 'Take your brush, put it in the paint and make a line across, a horizontal line...' and then 'Do it again, and then another, and another...'

We were a dozen in that place, and after half an hour we stopped and went round and looked at what people had done. My instructions were the same for everybody. There weren't two pictures that had the slightest connection - except that they had horizontal stripes.

I said 'Now that we are painters of horizontal stripes let's bring down all these papers and put another sheet up on the wall and let's paint vertical stripes.' When we finished I asked them 'What did you feel?' (since I did not know, I had to listen) and they said 'It's such a different experience. Your relationship to the same instrument and the same materials, the mere fact that you make it vertical instead of horizontal, it's an entirely different inner climate.'

We went back to the first drawings and we put them on the wall with the horizontal vertical and the vertical horizontal – which was a simple exercise – and you could see something about human beings, that human beings are vertical beings and their eyes are horizontal.

That is not for these people of the diplomatic corps; it's for everyone.

There was no intention of producing pictures that were worth looking at; it was teaching people to relate to themselves as capable of using colours and lines in any way. Anyone could have done the work I did with them. (1987b:8-9)

Here, Gattegno has removed any technical barriers the participants might have had: everyone can paint a straight line. As a result, the learners were only confronted with the questions that a painter must ask himself, undaunted by the prospect of executing the answers they find: How thick should this line be? How long? What is its relationship to the background if I paint it here, or here, or here? How would a line here affect the balance of the whole? Shall I make all the lines of the same length, and if not, what differences should I make? And so on.

For the time it took to do the exercise, participants would have been having cascades of awarenesses, very many of which would have been directed to the aesthetic effect that a painting makes on the person who looks at it. In the process of sorting these awarenesses out, participants were undoubtedly cultivating knowing in the way that a painter knows in his field.

## Knowing as a poet knows

Similar exercises can readily be devised for teaching other skills and subjects. In 1993, Bill Bernhardt and Peter Miller led a seminar on writing in Besançon which included the following paragraphs in its preamble:

> Writing has so often been considered as an art, skill or talent that only a very select few in any society feel confident enough to say, "I am a writer." Yet, at the same time, our daily lives are filled with writing activities addressed to ourselves, other individuals and institutions including: doodling and scribbling, signing documents, writing notes, diaries, poems, letters, essays, memoranda, faxes, business forms, wills, ... *What do we really know about ourselves as writers? How can we find out?*

> Writing has usually been studied and described through examining the language (vocabulary, syntax, style) of finished documents. Thus the process by which those texts were actually conceived, verbalized and transcribed, composed and edited, by an actual writer remained invisible. *What do we know about our own habits and ways of working as writers? How can we find out?*

In one of the exercises they set, participants were asked to write a poem using only words chosen from the 33 that appear on one of the Words in Color charts. (Since this is a programme to teach literacy, the words on the charts illustrate the spelling possibilities of English and are thus an arbitrary selection with respect to meaning.)

There were further constraints: that the poem should be just three lines long, with six, five and six syllables allowed in each line (similar to a Japanese haiku). Here are some examples:

See your mouth when you sleep
Fantastic question
When you sleep, see your mouth.

You, capable, quiet
Quiet, capable
Capable, quiet, you.

Once sleep quiets these feet,
Fantastic gardens
Phrase questions between doors.

As a participant, I (PM) can report that this exercise changed my relationship to writing. For an hour or so I was constrained in my possible vocabulary, in the number of feet and the number of lines I could use. So I was forced to weigh every word against every other. I tested the limits to which I could stretch English usage. I allowed nuances of meaning to preoccupy me.

The experience did not eventually push me into writing poetry, but for that hour I was operating as a poet. I was cultivating knowing as a poet must cultivate knowing in his field. Previously, I had never related to words, to word order, to the effect of one word upon another in the conscious and intense way that I did then. Since then, I have never written anything without these concerns being part of my writing.

### Knowing as a learner of language must know

The following example comes from the manual for a telephone English course. The exercises in this manual are procedures that are applied to written and spoken texts and images. They are 'empty', devoid of content, and thus suitable for students of all levels because it is the text they are applied to which determines their difficulty. It is possible to create exercises of this kind because all texts whatever their level have meaning and all contain nouns, verbs, articles, adverbs and adjectives.

The students work from a magazine, usually of their own choice. They are asked to buy two identical copies which will be the basis of the course; one copy is for the teacher, and the other for the student. The magazine must be related to a field they are interested in, professionally or otherwise.

The exercises are designed to involve students in work which will produce intuitions about the way English functions, as against giving them further knowledge of English. Here is an example.

Articles

Choose a story from your magazine. Underline each *the*, *a* and *an* in the story.

Make four lists of nouns in the story; those preceded by:

*the*
*a*
*an*
no article

What conclusions can you come to?

Can you move any of the nouns to a different group (e.g. 'a government' to 'the government')? What is the difference in meaning?

The students are directed towards an important and difficult part of the language. They are not given the rules that grammarians have developed to describe the usage of the articles. Instead, the exercise will provoke a series of awarenesses within a restricted domain and during a limited period of time, and this heightens the chances of making discoveries. The exercise will increase the students' sensitivity to the language.

Experiencing this cascade of awarenesses, the student is necessarily engaged in a process of knowing.

> Knowing is the form taken by awareness engaged in sorting out, in depth, the many demands of a complex activity that cannot be presented analytically and adequately by anybody. Knowing has the characteristic of intuition because both must respect the whole and find out, by the lightings provided by the self, what can be singled out to be retained, used, re-used, made automatic at a time one does not specifically know what is useful and worthwhile. (1976 V 5:6)

In teaching based on the transmission of knowledge, rather than knowing, the student is given the 'rules' (which become more complex as he goes from year to year) and asked to apply them. This, on its own, does not work. Those students who do master a subject after being taught this way, find a way to mobilise themselves spontaneously to do in an unstructured way what this exercise provokes in a clean, uncluttered way.

Once they realise the value of exercises of the kind above, many students are inspired to apply them more than once, to differing texts, thus building up a more complete and intuitive feel for the language.

### Knowing: epistemology or psychology?
One of the questions Gattegno asked himself was what discipline his work on knowing should fall into, epistemology or psychology.

Starting with epistemology, he noted that its definition differs from country to country. For the French, the Petit Robert Dictionary defines epistemology as "a critical study of the sciences, aimed at determining their logical origin, their value and their extent." In English, The Shorter Oxford Dictionary defines epistemology as "the theory of the method or grounds of knowledge."

Gattegno was very explicit in rejecting the French definition and proposed that epistemology should be the science of how we know. For him, we must study how mankind - all mankind - knows what it knows. He often quoted Goethe: "Every person is necessary if all human experience is to be lived". Every life is a human life and, if we want to know how humans know, we cannot afford to ignore anyone.

His vision of epistemology expands the scope of the discipline. For example, we can try to penetrate the ways of knowing of prehistoric man. Gattegno did this in 1984 during a seminar in the Dordogne region of France, where the participants visited the Lascaux caves and Gattegno subsequently described what he thought the painters were doing as humans living at that time.

Gattegno's epistemology also encompasses the evolution of each individual over a lifetime. He asked not only what adults do in order to know, but also what is done by the adolescent, by children, by new-born and by not-yet-born babies in order to know. He even asked what can be known by the self in the first cell.

> I see the boy and girl as epistemologists knowing what there is to know and how to achieve that knowledge as legitimately as Locke or Hume or Kant, or anyone else among those who asked themselves, 'What is there to know?' and embarked on finding a satisfactory answer. (1979 VIII 4:17)

Within psychology, cognitive psychologists investigate the internal mental processes of thought. However, in 1979 Gattegno protested that they were neither addressing knowing in childhood and before, nor recognising the role of affectivity. Their investigations were therefore too limited for a universal epistemology.

Having set himself the challenge of understanding learning, Gattegno never reduced the scope of this challenge to any simpler and more tractable form. He argued that it is always necessary to maintain complexity when one is studying a complex area. One must never simplify the question in the hope that everything can somehow be made simple and clear. If one does, one may no longer be studying a problem that is worth studying.

In seminars, when teaching others how to work on complex challenges, he often said: "Let yourself be educated by the problem!"

He made the same point in the introduction to *The Mind Teaches the Brain*, where he set out his general way of working:

I cannot study any question without seeing that it involves me and what I am at this moment, and that in order to respect the reality of the question I pose to myself, I have to let it reorganize myself until the question finds its place and is not reduced to what was already there. A place that transforms me.

Further, because I am in time, whenever I put a question to myself, it is a temporal question. I have to see what the question means for all the ages I have been and for myself when I have integrated all the lessons of the question.

To penetrate the reality of a question requires that the question penetrates my reality and that these movements between myself and the question have generated a dynamic that makes me know the question and makes the question be marked by me. ... Knowledge and knowing are inextricably intertwined. (1988a:6-7)

Gattegno, then, studied learning outside the discipline of psychology as it then defined itself, but located his work within what he believed to be the proper domain of this field.

I studied learning as a conscious act of a self endowed with many attributes such as awareness, will, intelligence, discrimination, retention, perception, imaging and so on. I became convinced that psychology could be defined as the science of time, the time we consume for experiencing. (1979 IX 2:8)

This is why the idea expressed in the citation at the beginning of Part 2 was so important to Gattegno: "Living a life is changing time into experience." Psychology then becomes the study of how each human being exchanges his or her time at conception into the experience they will have gained by the time of their death.

## Ways of knowing

There are more ways than one of arriving at the position where one can say, "I know." As soon as we realise this, it becomes important to identify the various ways of knowing and examine how they can lead to different kinds of knowledge.

The most complete presentation of the ways of knowing that Gattegno wrote is found in *The Science of Education*, although he was not attempting to provide an exhaustive list. He starts by placing the ways of knowing within the encompassing domain of awareness. "Behind all ways of knowing there is one self and its capacity to become aware." (1987a:56) Without an aware self, there would be no ways of knowing.

## Perception

Perception is a way of knowing that we apply to our environment, to ourselves and to our self. At the most basic level, what we perceive is changes in energy. The self perceives changes both in the level of energy, and in the attributes of energy. For example, it is through the perception of a range or spectrum of frequencies as well as their intensity that we perceive and recognise a pattern of energy that we experience as a sound.

Since perception deals with the reality of energy, it is at the basis of our sense of truth, the sense which informs us that we are in contact with reality. This is the foundation for all the mental activity we engage in. Perception is one of the direct ways of knowing (action is another). It does not usually require the spending of energy.

When one considers the cost of learning in terms of energy, it becomes clear that teachers can greatly reduce the price their students must pay if they base their work systematically on the students' powers of perception rather than on memorization, a very expensive way of learning.

If my students have their selves at the helm, then I can count on perception, the attribute of the self, to be at work. Affectivity will be providing all the energy needed for the work to be done, freely and naturally, without the students having to muster this energy. If I organise the class so that my students actively use perception, the way of knowing, then I introduce no obstacle to interrupt the learning process and my students will be left with the impression that their learning was cost free, easy and pleasant. More will be said on this in the next chapter, when we deal with the cost of memorization.

## Action

Action, together with the perception we have of action and its results, forms another direct way of knowing, creating another foundation for our sense of truth. The self mobilizes itself to bend some aspect of the outside world to its will, spends the energy to do this and recognises the results through perception as feedback from what it has done. This way of knowing is used extensively by small children who,

> ... test everything to become familiar with the attributes of hardness, softness, smoothness, slipperiness, roughness, resistance to effort, to tearing, to pulling, to pushing, to fitting, etc. (1987a:59)

How can a small child know what resistance will be offered by an object if he does not act upon it in order to find out? He is uninterested in its value for his parents. Its value for him lies in what he can discover about it by acting upon it. Thus he constructs his understanding of the world by means of action.

Later on, boys and girls use action in order to know themselves in their study of fine movements. As infants, they had torn paper to discover its resistance, and what they learned about was paper. Now, children learn from tearing and similar activities not about paper but about how best they should solicit their muscle tone.

As a further step, the evocation of movement opens the door to virtual actions which gradually reduce the need for actions to actually be performed. Virtual actions are actions which take place only in the mind. The advantages of the virtual world are that, firstly, the quantity of energy spent is incomparably less than that spent using muscles in the real world, and secondly, that the virtual world can be extended beyond the physical limitations that appear in the real one. When we fold sheets of A4 paper as an introduction to fractions, we are very soon restricted by the number of folds that are possible. It is our powers of virtual action that allow us to extend the exercise indefinitely, using and manipulating mental images.

> Hence, the preference of man for those actions that can be extended when they become virtual and which open the door to intellectual activities. (1987a:60)

## Analysis and synthesis
Analysis and synthesis are two ways of knowing derived from the blending of virtual (i.e. mental) action and perception. Analysis fragments, while synthesis uses perception and memory to create a new whole out of fragments. Gattegno recognised the importance of analysis as a way of knowing, since it is behind much scientific research, but insisted on the greater value of synthesis, which in his eyes was more important because it generates the great scientific discoveries as opposed to the routine research that accumulates scientific facts. To create a synthesis, the thinker juxtaposes facts and questions which to others have seemed to have no relation to each other and finds an overarching relationship.

> While analysis makes us aware of the content of any perception or notion, increasing our perception of attributes and of their number, synthesis makes us aware of what needs to be perceived behind the

appearances to note a unity hidden by the stressed differences. (1987a:64)

> A synthesis may suggest a new model instead of the current one, which holds together what is known so far while the new one includes that which could not be held by the previous one. This difference, in fact, is the only criterion for preferring one model to another. (1987a:64,65)

In the history of science, we see a recurring pattern where a thinker creates a synthesis and is followed by researchers who test and justify his vision using analysis. This pattern is found at more and less exalted levels, but in general the broader and more productive the synthesis, the greater the consequent renown of its originator.

Gattegno wrote at length of the value of synthesis in the sciences. In the field of chemistry, syntheses are "incomparably more difficult to perform than analyses." (1987a:65) In physics, the great names are those who have been able to synthesize in the field: Newton and Einstein, Faraday and Maxwell.

> In biology, the theory of evolution, the gene theory of heredity, the conception of the functioning of DNA and RNA, all represent mental syntheses that changed the overall grasp by man of what is essential and fundamental in the realm of the living. ... Syntheses are ways of making possible some thinking which is excluded by the endless fragmentation of analysis. (1987a:66)

He cites Darwin; Karl Marx who, "saw political evolution as the expression of economic interests fighting each other"; Sigmund Freud who, "saw all of our behaviors as the result of a few unconscious or subconscious drives struggling in the restricted area of our mind" (1987a:64); and many others (1982-1983).

Gattegno considered economics, meteorology and even geology to be disciplines which were not directed by an overall synthesis, but he pointed out that important work had been done in these fields at an analytical level in spite of the lack of a general unifying theory.

The presentation of a subject in a classroom must always rely on an analysis of the material by the teacher. She introduces the subject piece by piece, in lesson-sized chunks that she hopes will be assimilated by her students. However, the problems with this approach on its own are (1) that a school year or more might go by before the students gain a sense of the whole and (re)synthesize the subject from its parts, and (2) the teacher has no way of knowing when or even whether this has happened. The most she can do during the year is to identify some students who seem to have "cottoned on" while others remain "at sea".

These problems can be avoided if a clearly presented synthesis is in view even while analytical work is being done, since the students' vision of the whole then evolves while they are working on the details, and they learn to move freely from synthesis to analysis and to all the levels of complexity in between, from the tiniest detail to the overall goal. As a result, they know what they are doing: they understand the relationship of all the parts to one another and to the whole. The goal is always present, and provides a sense of direction and a measure of progress for the work being done. This closely reflects how people function outside a classroom.

Another way that a synthesis can be used to provide context for students is for the teacher to introduce a 'longitudinal' exercise from time to time. This will be a challenge that is constrained or simplified so that the students can be in contact with the whole subject even though they are not yet ready to deal with it in its full, real-life complexity.

> I (PM) vividly recall how I was taught contract law at university without such an approach, so that the work I did throughout the course only made sense at the end of the year. The lecturer may well have given an 'overview' of the course at the start, but at that point a synthetic presentation of this kind would have meant little, and if he did in fact give one I did not retain it. The year was spent analysing cases that turned on the minutiae of whatever aspect of a contract was being taught each week. Had the lecturer also spent a little time every few weeks presenting cases that spanned the whole topic, thereby demanding that students work on their syntheses of the subject, these would have created a proper context for the other work that we were doing.

> I was lost again for most of eight months I spent programming a dealing system for a foreign exchange trading company in the City of London. The system architect analysed the problem, and created program specifications for the programmers, who never understood how their work fitted into the whole until, at best, the end of the project. A few experiences, from time to time, where the programmers executed deals themselves as foreign exchange dealers (or at least shadowed real ones), and could thus have given themselves an evolving synthetic view of the overall problem, would have made the work we did on the frag-

ments of the project less prone to errors of interpretation and in this and other ways very much more effective.

We gave another example of this approach earlier, when we described how Gattegno taught painting. One of his exercises, painting horizontal and then vertical lines, eliminated the need for any expertise in drawing and thereby enabled the students to work on many of the other issues faced by a real painter: the harmony of elements on a page, the relationship of image to background, the numerous tints which can be obtained out of a single colour, etc. Each student had the experience of composing and executing several complete paintings within the space of a single day.

There is further potential in the deliberate use of synthesis. As a way of knowing it is enhanced by our power of evocation and the combination has remarkable force. Repeated reference to a visually presented synthesis, for example, quickly allows such reference to be made virtually, through the students' own evocation of the image. They are then using mental dynamics to retain the complex whole rather than memorising details. This is the kind of learning that can last a lifetime.

As will become clear in Volume 2, there are numerous examples of the deliberate use of synthesis in the materials created by Gattegno and others. The numeration table, the geoboard, the Animated Geometry films or Maurice Laurent's trigonometry board in mathematics; his grammar chart in the teaching of French grammar; the use of the Fidel, the sound/colour chart or the word charts in language teaching using Silent Way, Glenys Hanson's system for teaching the verb tenses of English and many other systems are all good examples of the coupling of analysis and synthesis. Their designers have demonstrated that if teachers work so that each student brings these materials to life by the powers of his or her self, then they become transformative teaching tools.

## Acquaintance

Acquaintance is the name Gattegno gives to both, "the kind of knowledge that the potter has of his clay, the painter of his paints, the musician of his instrument," and, for example,

> ... the way of knowing of two people who neither invest in each other, nor ever expect anything definite from each other, but who know they have access to each other and are ready to be further known. (1987a:68)

The first of these is illustrated in the accounts in Chapter 6 of Anne Laurent learning to use a Chinese inkbrush, and Christiane Rozet learning to throw a pot. The second might be illustrated by the acquaintance one gains of a colleague at work over a period of months and years. Common to both is a gradual amassing of many small and unexpressed awarenesses which, as they accumulate, create the experience from which we can say "I know how to throw a pot", or "I know Mark."

A teacher of pottery can choose a suitable clay, demonstrate the skill to be acquired and indicate pitfalls to avoid, so giving her student a way in to the craft of potting. The student's job is to do. While doing, he must be alert to all that the clay requires and allow the way it behaves in response to his movements to penetrate his awareness and shape his way of working. Although he is certainly engaged in an inner dialogue, he may very well not verbalize any part of it, either to himself or others[14]. Even when someone does use words, he could not express the whole process: it involves too many awarenesses following each other too rapidly. Each of these awarenesses moves fleetingly into his presence, affects him and then moves out, replaced by another. They cumulatively form him into someone who knows how to throw a pot.

> Acquaintance is a way of knowing used by all of us when we are conscious that familiarity is contributing something definite to what is experienced as familiar. Because of acquaintance with their instruments, musicians tune them at once and in the proper manner. Because of acquaintance, scientists know at once what is required of them when presented with a paper on a subject in their field. Everything familiar gains a concreteness that gives it relief and tells a great deal at once. The acquaintance with their field is what makes scientists more than analytic instruments. It makes them know what is relevant, what is important, what is significant and needs their attention. (1987a 69)

Acquaintance is certainly a very important way of knowing in the field of education. If it is, "the type of knowledge the potter has of his clay, the musician of his instrument, the artist of his paint," it is also the type of knowledge good students develop of a foreign language, if they are to speak it well. They need to master the particular energy distribution of that language as it is spoken, the pronunciation of the sounds, the pro-

---

[14] This is certainly the case for infants when they use acquaintance to come to know the world before they have language.

nouns, the verb tense system, the way the language enables human and spatial relations to be described, and so on. A teacher with this under-standing deliberately uses acquaintance as a way of knowing in her stu-students to enable them to build this complex core of the language. Rather than giving over precious time in the class to learning vocabulary, she ded-icates their time with her to the active construction of this core, the com-components of which are usually considered the most difficult. She does this by getting the students to create and say many, many examples of the core language in use. The vocabulary can then be added by the students without a teacher, as it would be by a native speaker.

Cecilia Bartoli drew an analogy between learning a language and learning the layout of a town one has just moved to. In both cases, it is efficient and human to learn by just 'walking around': becoming acquainted with the terrain.

Similarly, mathematicians must be acquainted with numbers.

> Some time ago, I (PM) was working with two young adults, Colin and Hussein, who are learning mathematics. Colin is developing his basic numeracy, and was working on division. Hussein is studying for A-level and was working on surds and indices.

> I realised that when Colin, Hussein and I look at a number we see very different things. For anything greater than about 10, Colin sees an undif-ferentiated 'lump', a discrete and arbitrary item. I, on the other hand, cannot see any number less than 100 without all its factors being pre-sent to me at the same time, and this is also true for many numbers greater than 100. So when I see 18, (3 x 6) and (2 x 9) are hovering in the periphery of my consciousness, as is (20 − 2). The number is anything but undifferentiated; rather it's a labile, unstable thing, ready to be replaced by its factors or some complementary pair at any moment.

> Hussein is somewhere between Colin and me. He showed by the way that he manipulates numbers that he experiences 25 as (5 x 5), but that he doesn't immediately see 75 as (3 x 25).

It is by consciously using acquaintance as a way of knowing in her stu-dents that a teacher of arithmetic enables them to know intimately that a number like 6 is not only the number which is after 5 and before 7, but also is (5 + 1), (4 + 2), etc; and also (7 - 1), (8 - 2), etc; and also (2 x 3) and (3 x 2), (1/2 of 12), (1/4 of 24) and (1/8 of 48), etc - so that 6 becomes a family of equivalences any one of which can be chosen as appropriate in given circumstances.

In fact, all school subjects can be deliberately thought through and restructured in such a way as to use acquaintance as a way of knowing in the students. The result is that they develop a deep and thorough understanding of the subject. Teachers need to return often to the question of how their subject can be presented so that students become acquainted with it, rather than accumulating knowledge which has no real link with the know-hows they need to build.

## Contemplation

Contemplation is a way of knowing in which we do not interfere with the object to which we are present.

> The self is aware of not being engaged in what it is knowing. The will is absent altogether because the self is reduced to and is maintained as a passive witness of what is ... When on a clear dark night, one looks at the stars, silent within and unrelated to anything else, then what one knows is known by contemplation. (1987a:71)

To reach a deliberate absence of will between one's self and what one seeks to understand is a movement of the mind, an act of the self.

Gattegno goes on to describe active uses of contemplation:

> Scientists who manage to contemplate what is accessible to them directly in their field, know that it is a way of knowing that gives them what they cannot obtain otherwise... Contemplation to them is a way of opening doors, a temporary phase in a way of knowing the world called ... 'the scientific method'. (1987a:71-72)

Further,

> When scientists present their findings, other scientists can see weaknesses in them that escaped the authors. This is not because of a better analysis but because beyond the analyses presented, there is a universe to which the various scientists have access. Contemplating that universe provides the means of seeing not only what the expounder saw but also something he did not see, which changes the perception and permits the criticism of the paper as well as providing a contribution beyond it. (1987a:72-73)

## Faith

At first sight, it might seem surprising that Gattegno included faith in his list of ways of knowing. But as he pointed out, faith is commonly used by everybody: the person who is not afraid to walk into a lift and press the button for the tenth floor knows that he can do this safely, and is using faith as his way of knowing. In the past, a supernatural being would have been for many people the most important locus of such a sense of trust, but nowadays our faith in the innumerable systems that we rely on every day - created by unknown architects, engineers and technicians - is probably more common.

It might also seem surprising to say that faith is present as a way of knowing in many classrooms. In fact, faith does have a legitimate place here. The teacher knows a certain number of things and the students can and should have faith in what she says and does, when it concerns those things.

The problem arises when the teacher asks her students to rely on faith for those parts of her teaching which should be based on other ways of knowing and on mental dynamics. The edifice that is then being constructed can only become more and more fragile as it grows. In such classes, faith takes up an inordinate place. When the teacher we described earlier asked his class to believe that $2 + 3 = 5$, he was asking of his students an act of faith, and in so doing was jeopardising their future in mathematics.

### Intuition

A definition of intuition as the word is commonly used might read something like this: "The faculty or process which gives us an ability to understand or know something without needing to think about it, to learn about it or to discover it by using reason." In the vernacular, an intuition, the output from this faculty, is sometimes called 'a hunch'.

Gattegno wanted to understand the process involved in intuition and also the intuitions thus generated. He therefore examined what takes place within ourselves when this is the word we use to describe this way of knowing. He found that the key characteristic of intuition is that the self maintains contact with the whole: the whole field, the whole situation, the 'big picture'.

Present to the whole, the self may note either what comes to it immediately, in a flash, or what comes to it as it simply stays in contact with the whole: a growing understanding of a situation which leads to an awareness - "it dawned on me." In both these cases, we say that what we know has come to us intuitively.

In a seminar that Gattegno led in 1974, he described an everyday situation in which intuition and other ways of knowing could be studied: a mother who looks at her child one morning and puts her hand on his forehead to check if he has a fever. Her general impression of the whole of the child tells her that something is wrong, but no one clue is sufficiently outstanding for her to be certain. The test for a fever is temperature, and the most immediate way to establish this is by putting her hand on the child's forehead.

It is clear that action and perception were the way she tested her hypothesis, but what way of knowing led her to know that something was wrong if no one clue established this? None of the ways of knowing discussed above adequately explains her knowledge. Intuition was the word Gattegno chose for the way of knowing involved here, the result of being in contact with the whole of her child, a way of knowing which is common in everyday life.

Once recognised, intuition can be legitimised as a way of knowing, and used intentionally. While present to the whole, the self may actively investigate it, deliberately lighting it in different ways, stressing and ignoring by highlighting certain aspects and casting others into shadow. By using a number of lightings, one knows more and more about the area being investigated. This may happen over a period of a few seconds or many years.

Gattegno's use of the word 'intuition' can thus be seen to have a meaning that relates to how the word is commonly used, but which captures the process as well as the outcome. The key characteristic, maintaining contact with the whole, is common to both usages.

When intuition provides an overall framework for an investigation, other ways of knowing will also be used within this. Conversely, when other ways of knowing have been brought in to investigate a question, it can be profitable to resituate the question within a framework of intuition so as to deliberately solicit various lightings on it.

> Every time we give ourselves the task of grasping a 'universe of experience' we somehow know that we are unable to say that we are in contact with it unless we feel that we maintain an awareness of the presence of the whole even while we work on part of it.

> For example, if we want to know love, friendship, affectivity, the mind, the self, etc., we must make sure that the presence of each as a whole is with us while we experience our movements for knowing it better through lightings of that whole which do not exhaust the whole.

> Intuition is this dual awareness of the self carefully holding the whole and seeing in it this or that. The self recognizes by this deliberate respect of the presence of the whole that the way of knowing being used at that moment maintains the whole in the awareness. This is essential for intuition to be at work. (1975c:2)

One of Gattegno's books, *The Mind Teaches the Brain*, is a good example of the use of intuition as a way of studying a complex phenomenon. In this book, he examines the mind using different lightings, as is immediately clear from the table of contents. Each of the 16 chapters lights the subject from a different viewpoint: The Amorous Self, The Perceptive Self, The Intelligent Self, The Symbolizing Self, The Relating Self, The Moral Self, etc. Even this, of course, is far from a complete study. However, it illustrates well how maintaining a whole – the whole of our human experience – and deliberately lighting it from many different points of view, yields new insights into the relationship between the mind and the brain.

> Intuition, singled out here for our purpose, differs from all the above but, like all the above ways of knowing, is compatible with them. The self acknowledges that it differs because it connects with the whole, maintains the whole, respects its presence at the same time as the self perceives, acts, transforms, fragments, unites, etc.

> Intuition is the way of the self knowing itself as active in not letting the impact of the whole be moved out of awareness and noting what it does to that awareness at work.

> When people deliberately stress this or that way of knowing but not intuition, they may not know that intuition is also at work. Indeed at the subconscious level intuition must be at work to tell the knower that the work done is within the initial challenge.

> Intuition may be stressed or not stressed by the self. This does not mean that it is not doing its work all the time, whatever the state of the observer. We all need it and use it, even when we do not suspect its existence.

> But intuition can come into its own and gain a new importance as an instrument of the self and provide means of working on what cannot be tackled by perception, action, analysis or the others. Those who cultivate intuition have at their disposal aspects of truth and reality which escape others. In particular only intuition can handle complexity ... Intuition, although it is not everything, has or could have, an important place in everyone's life. (1975c:3)

Readers can now better understand the way that Gattegno presented the attributes of the self, discussed in Chapter 2. Each of 'the attributes' had to be highlighted in turn, but intuition allowed us to stay in contact with the fact that these are attributes 'of the self'.

And just as when one attribute comes to the fore in real life, this does not imply that this attribute alone is functioning, so the ways of knowing combine and intermingle in response to the task at hand:

> All these ways of knowing are at work in every one of us at different levels, different moments, and in different combinations. (1975c:3)

**Further reading**

*The Science of Education Part 1*

*De l'intuition*

# 8   On memory

Gattegno presented the results of his reflections on memory in two books, *Evolution and Memory* and *The Science of Education*. One of his conclusions, one that is particularly relevant for education, was that it is necessary to make a distinction between memorisation and what he called 'retention' to account for how we stock and use our past.

However, his thinking on memory encompassed its place in the whole of the universe as well as its role in human functioning. The last sentences of *Evolution and Memory* read, "Memory is no more than the objectified world. Nor less." (1977a:87) In Gattegno's vision, there are examples of memory functioning everywhere in the universe. This is so much the case that one could almost say that the universe *is* memory. For example, DNA can be understood as one of the ways nature gave itself in order to retain a memory of what it has done. The notion of valency in chemistry can also be understood in terms of memory.

However, this chapter will only deal with memory as it functions in humans, and even so will not deal with all the facets of human memory that Gattegno explored.

## The nature of memory ...

Gattegno set the stage by stating that any serious study of memory had to take all of the following aspects of it into account (1987a: 177-180):

> Our memory is not made of a single component, does not have just a single attribute, although when we always use the same word for memory we may have the tendency of wanting it to be one thing only. Memory, in fact, is an open set of features and properties, many things being considered together but capable of being considered separately.

> It can appear as coextensive with our lives.

It is with us all our lives. It allows us to recognize facts, situations, circumstances we have lived. Memory is completely personal. My memory can only be mine.

It can appear as having different attributes at different times of our lives.

If we study memory at different periods of one life - *in utero*, during childhood, at adolescence, at the period of life we call 'middle age' and in old age - it has different characteristics. Further, our relationship to memory in the waking state is different from our relationship to memory during sleep.

It can appear as having different properties when we consider that some memories are images, some are emotions or feelings, some are ideas, some are capable of becoming social entities, like institutions.

It can appear as handling energy in different ways when we attempt to retain a poem, a song, a piece of music, etc., and succeed.

It can appear as stable and fleeting at the same time: fleeting because of the nature of its substance when we reach it, stable in that it can be recalled many times and be recognized as being the 'same.' In forgetting, we know its 'fleetingness'; in its responsiveness to our recalls, its stability.

It can appear as nothing and everything; nothing since it does not normally have weight and has its own dynamics of disappearance and reappearance; everything because without it we have no means of understanding our integrity, our wholeness, which is the equivalent of our existential being.

It can appear as the objectivation of time.

In saying this, Gattegno was expressing in another manner his 'equation'[15]: "to live a life is to change time into experience." At conception, the only thing we have at our disposal is the content of the first cell and a lifetime ahead of us, which might be measured in just days or in decades. At the end of our life, we have no more time but we have gained experience. This perspective allows us to see why Gattegno defined psychology as "the science of time." (1967:139)

---

[15] He used to joke that every self-respecting mathematician invents an equation, and that this was his.

> [Memory] can appear as not only made of memories but of their dynamics, those which link memories, those which activate them, those which deactivate them.

Our memories are not distinct from each other. There are connections between them which are an integral part of memory and which can be acted upon independently. Mental imagery is an illustration of how we use the dynamics of memory.

> [Memory] can appear as one's past, but not a past attached rigidly to a chronological line which gives a date to so many memories. A past that can be studied and thus gain a new significance and a new meaning, its reality neglected by the urge to live the present and project the future.

Here, then, Gattegno insists on the fact that the past is labile.

> Because of the awareness that memory is one's past - and one's past, enlivened singularly and idiosyncratically, is one's memory - new challenges in this field can surface up and ask to be treated and understood. The names of some of these challenges are retention, recognition, evocation, local and global organizations of memories, the meanings attached to them. The contents of dreams, the contents of one's psyche, are some others.

For Gattegno, any theory of memory must account for all these aspects of memory.

## ... and the nature of one's past

### The new integrates the old
If we consider how our memory comes into existence, it may seem obvious that our present experiences are simply added to our stock of memories. I live a day and the memories for that day are added to those of the previous days and years of my life. However, for memory to serve us easily, silently and fluently, it must be an integrated whole. Given the sheer extent of our past, it might seem common sense to assume that what we have already lived integrates what we have just lived, that is, that the old integrates the new, but a model of simple addition does not show us how this is achieved.

Gattegno proposed the opposite – that the new integrates the old: the newly met dominates all our previous experience which the self integrates into it. Sleep is what gives us the opportunity to do this. Thus during each period of sleep, the awarenesses that have emerged during the previous waking state are used by the self to recast all that previously existed, so that we wake up modified by the previous day's experience, sometimes very profoundly. Gattegno reached this conclusion by asking himself the question: "How can we account for conversions?"[16]

## Conversions

The word 'conversion' is usually associated with major life changes, but as Gattegno pointed out, we all live many conversions throughout our lives. One such conversion happens in the playground when, overnight, skipping takes the place of hopscotch. For little girls, living their lives intensely in the absolute of action, this change is a conversion. The child who is now skipping is the 'new' child, who has cut off the flow of energy which was her previous passion for hopscotch, retaining only the know-hows she developed. She is now committing as much energy as circumstances will allow to her new passion for skipping. She is, this morning, the result of her night's sleep, the result of her most recent conversion.

The example of taking up windsurfing in Chapter 6 is also a conversion. The learner sees this new way of using himself and immediately becomes someone whose life has a place in it for windsurfing. It now occupies the time previously taken by other activities which seem (if he were prompted to think about them) to have simply vanished from his mind.

Learning to eat black olives which one previously detested can also be considered a conversion, though of a slightly different kind. The energy sustaining the previous refusal to eat them is psychic energy. The self must now deploy energy in the form of a willingness to test the taste of black olives for a second 'first time'. It must be alert to the ease with which the psyche could interrupt the trial and hold it at bay by remaining at the helm throughout the whole 15 second process.

As we begin to see the role in our lives of conversions large and small, it becomes clear that if there is a change in the way we choose to relate to the world, or if there is an awareness in Stage 1 of the learning process which has led to a change in the way we spend our time, then a conversion has taken place. However, it is clear that although conversions are always the result of awarenesses, most awarenesses do not lead to conversions.

---

[16] We will see in the next chapter that the notion of the new integrating the old and subordinating it is not limited to the domain of memory. It is found in many domains.

Conversions are of the realm of the self and are a sign of growth. When we live a conversion, it is the self which converts and all the modifications that are needed to accommodate the new vector in our lives appear to ripple very easily through the psyche. Thus in conversions it is particularly clear that the new integrates the old, but Gattegno contended that this is true for every aspect of our lives and that it can be no other way.

As we saw in Chapters 3 and 5, we give ourselves automatisms to free the self, allowing it to move on to new learning. However, if the self makes no use of this freedom then it is the psyche alone which directs our lives and conversions cease. We are then no longer actively creating our lives, but being lived. This is how life becomes humdrum.

### Can I change my past?

There is another aspect of memory where Gattegno's thinking runs counter to what the common belief about the relationship we have to our past might seem to be. He observed that this relationship is not essentially a relationship to the fixed record of what has been lived, the sequence of events. Rather, our past constantly changes as a result of our capacity to recall it and reinvest in it.

This was the central point of a seminar led by Gattegno in Geneva in 1979 called *Peut-on changer son passé?* ('Can one change one's past?'), where the conclusion reached was not only that we *can* change our past, but that we cannot *not* change our past (if we are to remain mentally healthy). There is no need for active intervention for this: the simple fact of calling up a memory modifies it. A memory emerges into the present of what we are now, which includes the experience we have gained since the memory was last recalled. In this way, dozens upon dozens of memories are overlaid and knit together; in particular for people and places we know well.

Not only this, but we also create 'memories'. We can easily have two or more memories of the same event, of which one is the 'real' one and the others are constructions seen from an outsider's viewpoint, as if we were a spectator at the scene. These other memories are constructed from the rest of our experience.

> From when I was six, I have two memories of an incident where I was on a narrow path leading to a level crossing over a railway line. In the first, I am close to a train moving by me at high speed. I remember being sucked towards the passing train and I can still see the train a few inches in front of me. My brother who was standing behind me put his hand on my shoulder and gently steadied me. In the second memory I have of

this same incident, I see the scene from overhead. I can see the little girl dressed in blue as she drifts towards the train speeding by.

This second memory is clearly a construction.

> I also have two entirely different memories of a heated argument in which I was once involved. In one, I can see myself from a place near the ceiling, watching the argument in which I was participating. In the second memory of this same argument, I am where I was, and I can still evoke the emotional state I was in, but I cannot hear the voices. The second memory comes to the surface only with difficulty. When I evoke this scene, it is the first memory which comes to mind spontaneously, a memory which is devoid of emotion.

How is it that these two memories co-exist in me? That one is devoid of emotion while the other contains no voices? For what reason(s) do I have two memories of the same event?

> I 'remember' being thrown out of my pram when I was only six months old. I do not see the pram turn over from where I was, inside it. What I see is what an adult watching the event from a few metres away would have seen: the pram turning over and me falling to the ground. This memory is entirely constructed. I have no real memory of this incident, although I have been told that it happened to me.

These examples demonstrate a few of the ways in which we change our past and why this needs to be taken into account when we try to understand what memory is.

## How do we generate our past?

For Gattegno, the past is generated by the movement from one awareness to the next in the succession of awarenesses we live as we go about our lives. As I become aware, I leave behind the awareness I have just had, and I know that, because it is no longer the awareness to which I am present, it now belongs to my past. This is how I generate my past, and know that I am doing it.

> I get into a very crowded bus. I have to twist my body in order to fit between all the people around me. I know I will not be able to hold this stance until the end of the trip. I urgently need to find a better place to put my other foot down before the bus gathers speed or, worse still, brakes suddenly. Because there are so many bags on the floor, I must find a place to slide my foot down between them. I glance at the different bags and my neighbours' legs, estimate the chances of making a

space for my foot and realise that if I push this bag here just a little, I should be able to get my foot to the floor. I push the bag, feeling its resistance and being aware of how this is a combination of its weight and its contact with the other bags and legs around it. Finally I get to the point where I can slide my foot down to the floor. I move my body and test the new position. If I estimate that I will be able to stand like this for the rest of the journey, I resign myself to the lack of comfort, and wait, alert to the movements of the bus and aware of the need to hold more firmly onto a strap if it brakes. If I allow my presence to move away from my balance, there is every chance I will find myself beginning to fall.

Awareness after awareness; dozens have succeeded each other in the time it took for me to find a place where I could stand safely; awarenesses related to the on-going challenge of remaining upright as well as all the other awarenesses that I had.

Each time a new awareness takes place in our mind, it takes the place of the previous awareness to which we are therefore no longer present. What is not in our present already belongs to our past. Thus, instant by instant, awareness after awareness, we constantly generate our past.

The next time I sleep, this journey will integrate the whole of my experience of the activity of bus-taking.

## Retention and memorisation

Gattegno identified retention, recognition, evocation and memorization as among various distinct aspects of what people call 'memory'. He described them and the differences between them in terms of how they use energy. As we shall see, one key awareness for teachers is that retention and memorisation are different processes, with different costs, with different outcomes and which can be engaged in students by their teachers for more or less effective learning.

### Retention

Our memories of places, of melodies, of the quality of a voice and so on, tell us that we have the capacity to retain such structured energy. They tell us that energy which has impinged on our sense organs can be retained without any conscience attempt or effort to make this happen. Our system has simply been affected by a movement of energy and some effect has persisted.

> A few years ago, I went back to a small French village that I had not vis-
> ited for fifteen years and I knew immediately: "Of course! The bakery is
> over there behind the butcher's shop," and I knew that I was right. The
> bakery was where I knew it would be. If I hadn't found it, I would have
> said to myself, "Oh they've moved it!" rather than "Oh, I've made a mis-
> take."

When I am in a supermarket and I notice someone else, I can recognize
him or her some minutes later a few aisles further along. I know that it is
the same person; there can be no doubt.

In my car on the motorway, during long journeys, I can often say that a car
that overtakes me has overtaken me some time earlier on the trip.

It is retention which allows all these feats of memory. None of them cost
us anything. They happen if we are present to our surroundings.

> Retention can be looked at quantitatively and qualitatively. There is a
> meaning in which one can say, 'I retain more now than I did earlier'
> – for example, when we learn to be 'more present' in our perceptions
> and let more of the components of the energy which reaches us to be
> perceived as belonging to the perception. Looking at a landscape or
> at a picture would be good illustrations. That sort of presence can be
> cultivated and made second-nature and is applicable to all areas in
> which one's awareness is at work. Then one retains <u>more</u> because one
> sees <u>more</u>, and one <u>sees</u> more because one is <u>more</u> present.
>
> On the qualitative side, retention can be said to be purer when the
> self is watchful of the distractions which take away some of the pres-
> ence needed to increase retention quantitatively. Because of the
> purer quality of what is retained, the self is more confident that what
> is in oneself does belong also to the source of the energy received.
> (1987a:183)

Gattegno noted two further aspects of retention, namely recognition and
evocation.

## Recognition

Given something that we now perceive, we need to know whether we have
met it before or not. It would be costly if we had to mobilise enough energy to generate the whole of the original in order to answer this question.
Recognition has been developed by the self to be an economic device by
which a subtler form of the original or a part of it becomes sufficient to
generate full awareness of the whole.

The arena of recognition is awareness; the purpose of the exercise is to substitute awareness of parts for awareness of wholes, ending with the self securely confident and in command, even though less energy is involved in recognition than would be used if the wholes needed to be present to generate awareness. (1987a:185)

I am walking down the main street of my city one day and I think I recognise a person that I worked with for a few days recently. I need to walk up beside him and look at his face before I can be sure.

Another time, on a cold winter's day, I get a glimpse through the crowd of a person well wrapped up like everyone else, who I nevertheless immediately recognise as my friend John.

These examples illustrate that ever more subtle forms of the original can be generated which will still allow one to recognise the whole.

Since [recognition] is a deliberate move of the self, practiced through all one's life, each of us becomes expert in placing on top of one set of objectivations another set issued from it but formed of less expensive fractions of energy. The link with the earlier set exists because the new one can trigger it as soon as it is needed. ...

The temporal hierarchy of the successive substitutions of recognizable entities from earlier ones corresponds to the mental evolution of Man, and covers the generation of symbolism and the layering of more and more comprehensive symbols which appear more and more abstract, except to the expert of the alerted minds. Mathematics is the best known example of such workings of the mind. But it can be found in many other fields, from language use to linguistics, from rules of movements of chess pieces to masters' contests, from returning a ball in a tennis game to forecasting where a volley will land, and so on. (1987a:186-187)

## Evocation

Evocation is the attribute of the self that enables it to call up all kinds of images that have been previously retained, to examine them and act upon them.

While memory is being structured through retentions and recognitions, it becomes an entity the self can use ... Once we reach that stage, we can reverse the process and meet another attribute of the self which we can study under the name of <u>evocation</u>. The material of evocation is always some retained material... The self selecting some retained material can reactivate it into consciousness. This is called evocation. (1987a:188)

> I am in my study when I realise I should go shopping. I make my list by evoking both what I have in the house and what is in season; I can see in my mind's eye what was in the shop the last time I was there. (The expression 'in my mind's eye' is another way of speaking of evocation.) I also consider the recipes that I might make in the next few days and construct meals around them by evoking their tastes. I mentally go around the cupboards and the fridge making sure that the ingredients are available. Occasionally I am unable to evoke whether I have enough of what I need and I must check. I also evoke the shop I am going to, and organise my list according to its layout.

We can act on what we are evoking without changing the energetic structure of the initial retained form. Indeed, we often transform the image while maintaining the original form beside it, working with both of them, alternating between them. Thus evocation can be a complex movement.

To understand, and experiment with, the difference between receiving energies from outside and evoking, one need only look at an object for a few minutes, being attentive to its details, and then close one's eyes to evoke what has been looked at. For most people, the new image loses in colour because they have not educated their capacity to evoke colour. It loses in precision because we only see what we think will be necessary, and only retain what we have seen (probably a small fraction of what an artist might have seen, and far less than we know is there), and we can then only evoke what we have. An evocation is often more like a sketch than a picture.

When we look at an object, the apparatus and automatisms of vision furnish us with an image which has no cost to the self, whatever the quality of image required. To evoke, the self must draw on affective energy to create a new image. This, too, is cost free unless we demand more from the evocation than would be needed for simple recognition.

## Memorization
Living a life is changing time into experience. When I am present to what I do and this is contributing to my experience, it can be retained.

Memorization is different from retention. It is needed because it is sometimes necessary to hold and recall things that can have no basis in our experience and which for us, therefore, are arbitrary.

When we meet John we may start to experience the person, but his name is arbitrary. He could have been called Peter. This is why we so often recognise a person – drawing on what we have retained – but are unable to find his name, which had to be memorised.

Magna Carta could have been signed in 1214 or 1216. The fact that it was signed in 1215 has to be memorized by anyone unfamiliar with the reign of King John. In order to memorize such a fact, Gattegno described how we have to mobilise a special amount of mental energy to 'glue' Magna Carta and 1215 together. He realised that we need a name for the unit of energy each single operation of this kind requires, and called it an 'ogden'[17], understanding that once a notion has been separated in one's awareness then labelling it gives it greater prominence. This mental 'gluing' has a cost. Indeed, memorisation can be very costly.

> We pay ogdens to remember what we cannot generate by ourselves, the situation in all cases of natural retention ... The process of paying ogdens has been called, for some time, memorization. This is an artificial way of retaining, following its own laws and prone to 'forgetting'.

> If we are careful and indeed pay the ogdens, we can remember the arbitrary and make it look as if it were as good as natural retention. It is not, and the dynamics of ogdens remains an open field of investigation.

> What we want to stress here is the difference between natural retention, an attribute of the mind, the source of true memory, and memorization, a forced device to obtain retention in the case of arbitrary associations.

> Learning based on retention is, by definition, integrated and may last forever; retention based on memorization may have a very different

---

[17] Gattegno recounted that in 1971 he was sitting in a plane talking about memorisation to his neighbour who, by asking him what the unit of energy was called, prompted Gattegno to immediately give it his neighbour's name. Stevick (1990:118) reported that the ogden was named after the British polymath C.K. Ogden, but Ogden died in 1957, and we assume instead that Gattegno's neighbour was Ogden Lindsley since there are several sources showing that each knew - and appreciated - the other's work.

destiny, cannot be called true learning and is often forgotten, sometimes very soon after the attempts at paying the requested ogdens.

At least we now have the language to distinguish two processes found
around us and rarely carefully disentangled. Memorisation leads to
the awareness of forgetting and forgetfulness, retention does not
produce them. (1987a:198)

Although the string of sounds making up a word in any language is entirely arbitrary, and must therefore be memorised, the association between
string and meaning must have been direct when the word itself was invented, and is direct again whenever the word is learnt in the mother
tongue. "Curtain," for example, will be noticed by a child in someone else's
speech when he experiences an event which involves curtains. The arbitrary string of sounds is glued to the vivid concept of a curtain, such as he
then has it. The cost of this ogden is not overwhelming, and memorisation
will be secured by the regular reappearance of this word[18].

This is very different from learning the French word *rideau* as part of a
word list. In this case, a learner is being invited to glue one word to another word rather than to glue the word to the concept of a curtain which has
been brought into present awareness through lived experience.

The great majority of learners, who do the task that they have been set,
rapidly experience this type of memorisation as an oppressive waste of
time: to begin with, as an exercise with an overwhelming cost, paid to try
to glue together two items both of which are arbitrary and which have no
reason to be joined, and then, as the disappointment felt soon after when
the learner realises that the glue has not held[19].

This futile activity is called learning by rote, and the pity of it is, that even
for those who do memorise the word *rideau*, little in fact has been gained.
When confronted with the need to produce the word, it will not present
itself spontaneously since the word is not glued to the concept, and the
speaker will be forced to stop and look for the word, having no option but
to resort to the roundabout method of word retrieval of going via English.
This leads to the result that people who had good marks in French for four

[18] "Retention results both from the payment of ogdens and from practice. Man is a retentive
system and there is no need to worry specially about forgetting thousands of words met in
topical situations. If words do not come easily when needed, it is either because the payment
of ogdens has not been attended to as required, or because the topic is not so frequent that it
offers opportunities for reuse." (1985:74)

[19] 3/10 in French vocabulary, after all that work last night!

or five years can nevertheless be incapable of holding a conversation in the language.

However, the retention of new material need not be so costly. Even learning that could be arbitrary can be recast by teachers in ways that are adapted to how humans learn and how memory functions. Gattegno gives the following example.

> A poem ... is an integrative schema which holds together each word or line or verse ..., first in local organizations and then in a larger one, integrating every item by subordinating it to do the job of the whole. Memory function works like this because it is in this way that it has been generated. ... Hence, [memory's] evolution tells us how to acquire a poem ... by structuring our time to display the law of integration and subordination[20]. ...

> The result seemingly can be described as memorization - meaning rote learning through drill and repetition - when in fact, it is the work of integration which generates its reality and its presence in our memory. We call the learning of a poem memorization, but in fact we use our sensitivities, our intelligence, our sense of truth and aesthetic sense, to make a whole of it and to be helped by that whole to retain the poem globally and then locally, so as to be able to unroll it as a structuration of time through energy. ... The self can recall it, as a string of evocations, one helping the other to come forward and take its place. The well-knit sequence is replaced by one whole in which both the elements themselves and the order of their appearances are dictated by the integrative schema. (1987a:194-195)

## Forgetting

> In the brain, memory is nothing if it is not perceived as dynamic and not seen in its reality, that is, with all the components of holding, releasing, eliminating. No one can think of memory without considering forgetting. We all feel right when we remember something but astonished that such-or-such a thing is forgotten. We know ourselves as capable of retention, of retaining a great deal, and we consider forgetting what we once knew as a dysfunction. (1988a:156)

Gattegno spoke of the memory as "the organ for forgetting." In saying this, he made us aware that there is no end to the things we forget. What did I eat for my midday meal on November 26th, 1998? 1988?

---

[20] This law is explained at the beginning of the next chapter.

> [I]n a changing world one discovers that the ability to forget is need-
> ed as much as the capacity to retain and that there is no value in
> taking the time to fix in one's mind what no longer obtains. No one in
> such a world is prepared to pay a heavy price for what is no longer
> functional. (1971:6)

For example,

> In January 2009 I stayed in a hotel in Paris for two nights. In my mind's
> eye I can see the entrance to the hotel, the desk and the lift, and I can
> find my way to my room on the third floor. But I have absolutely no idea
> what the number on the door was.

What I retained through images remains, at no cost. On the other hand,
the energetic structure I created to retain the room number by memorisation has been dissolved. The energy I fed it with for the period of my stay
is no longer required.

We can also lose a word, even a word we have known for a long time and
which is quite familiar, and we say, "It's on the tip of my tongue ..." The
way the word becomes available again informs us that words are not
stocked in what we normally call 'memory', a place that we can actively
search. This is why we come to realise that if we stop looking, it will come
back to us.

Even in the place that we normally call memory, things do not happen in
quite the way we would expect. For example, Gattegno was struck by what
can happen after one has learnt a song:

> Selective forgetfulness is one of the functions of the mind. The mind
> can manage to forget one item linked to many others, to separate, as
> it does in the case of songs, what was never separated to begin with
> and recall either the words or the tune or a mixture of separate ele-
> ments. The self knows what is stored, but it does not always know
> just how to bring back what is resisting recall. (1988a:167)

We can lose names and dates. However, it is necessary to be clear about
what 'lose' means in this situation. It does not mean that what we are
looking for is no longer in us, but only that no automatised path to it functions at present. With the right trigger, things do come back.

We also need to distinguish between things which can be forgotten and
things which were never destined to be remembered:

> When I was seven, I learnt to ride a bicycle. I remember almost falling off into brambles. I remember losing control and crashing into a palm tree. What I remember are the emotionally charged incidents which took place over the same period as the learning process.

> I have no memories of what I actually did to learn to ride but I must have learnt so many things: to push alternately on each pedal, to develop my balance, to discover how much to lean for turning a corner, to coordinate turning the handlebars with the leaning, and so on.

If pressed to say *how* they learnt to ride a bicycle (strictly the process, excluding the anecdotes), people would normally say that they have forgotten. Gattegno proposed that in learning skills, the skill finally acquired *is* the memory, so we should normally expect to retain no 'memories' of the process. (Note that once one becomes aware of the nature of the learning process, one learns to observe one's awarenesses as events, and these can then be remembered.)

Forgetting also gives us a lighting on the apparently smooth and unified system that each of us is, in most of our functionings.

> We all forget. So, we can all find opportunities of being face to face with a gap where what was once energized is not now recallable. ... [W]e sense the duality of the searching self and the thing [to be] remembered, a duality [normally] fused into a continuous and undistinguishable whole which suddenly breaks apart into two components: one, the self, having as its present function to look for an item which it knows belongs to it ... and the other, the forgotten item, — part of the self's objectified world. These two sensations ... accompany the shock and the awareness that one cannot recall what was once one's own. (1978a:22)

Finally, Gattegno was very aware that he was far from having solved all the problems that memory poses:

> The mystery of memory and its diverse functionings remains almost as great after all this study as at the start, but something is certainly clearer: that only by recognizing the complexity of the workings of the mind and the complex dynamics within it, on top of the intricacies of the brain, shall we be in a position to penetrate the universe of memory a little. (1988:167)

## Further reading

*The Science of Education* (especially Part I, Chapter 5)

*Evolution and Memory*

*La mémoire*

# Part III

# Where do we come from?

"From your window you see a sight which delights you. You can ask yourself: How can I understand all this in terms of energy? ... energy is everywhere, energy is everything ..."

Caleb Gattegno, *L'énergie et les énergies*, Vol.I, page 15

# 9 The four realms – from the Big Bang to human beings

## The starting hypothesis

As he worked on his energy-based description of humans living their lives, Gattegno realised that he could go further; that the ideas of Einstein and Darwin would enable him to develop an account of evolution that could begin with the Big Bang and encompass all human activity.

If Einstein is right, the whole universe is energy, transmuted or not into matter. And if Darwin is right, the living world is part of a process of evolution. Gattegno combined and extended these ideas to propose that at the most fundamental level, it is energy itself that evolves.

He described two laws and an axiom. He found that these operate everywhere in the universe. The first law is that of subordination by integration, the second is that of economy of energy. The axiom is that of temporal hierarchies.

## Subordination by integration

The phenomenon of subordination by integration has been well known to biologists and neurologists since the turn of the twentieth century. They find it, for example, in embryonic development, where successive strata of the brain and spinal column are put into place, each layer being subordinated to the one which succeeds it, with this new one integrating the functioning of the older one. The result is a form of hierarchical control, illustrated by what happens when the head is cut off a chicken yet it runs around for some time afterwards. The layers of brain which inhibit running reflexes have been removed, releasing the running behaviour.

According to Marcault and Brosse (1939) and Gattegno following them, this principle is not only seen in biology. It also applies to the psychological development of man including the general structure of learning. And as we shall see, Gattegno further applies it to the evolution of energy. For him, it is a universal law manifesting itself whenever energy evolves into a new form. It defines the manner by which such changes take place: every time there is an evolutionary change, the new subordinates the old by integrating it.

A corollary of this law is that the process of evolution is not simply additive. When it is the case that the old integrates the new - that is, that the new is made to conform to the old and assimilated into it - then this is rightly seen as an additive process. Psychotic behaviour is an example of this. All new experience is assimilated into the psychosis and buttresses it, and evolution stops.

But the meaning of the law of subordination by integration is that the new subordinates the old by integrating it. What has already been created passes directly under the control of what is now being created; the old can now only express itself in a way which is compatible with the new, a way which does not disturb the integrity of the whole, governed as this now is by the new.

Once learning has been integrated, the learning process itself disappears; what is left is the product. Gattegno pointed out that the reason why we have so few memories of our early childhood is that we were learning know-hows, and each know-how is the memory of the time spent on learning it. This explains why small children, when asked what they did during the day at kindergarten, usually reply, "Nothing." Throughout the day they are actively creating know-hows, and this does not leave anything that can be recounted later.

Integration, then, is a complex process which requires the remodelling of the whole so that integration by anything new produces a new whole, richer than the preceding whole.

In Gattegno's proposals for understanding the evolution of the universe, the law of subordination by integration is seen operating at each new level.

**Economy of energy**
Gattegno further proposed that everywhere in the Universe evolution is a systematic search for ever more economic functionings, both in time and in energy. He often summed this up by saying simply "more for less": the 'more' being more productivity and the 'less' being less time or energy - or both - needed to be spent in order to obtain a given result. In Man, this proposal expresses itself as a highly developed sense of economy which pervades all aspects of human life, and always has done. Almost every

man-made item – from water pipes to trays to shopping lists, from the domestication of animals to all forms of transport – demonstrates man's sensitivity to 'yield', to the relationship between what one gets and what one spends to get it.

### Temporal hierarchies

Some events must take place in an order and this creates what Gattegno calls a 'temporal hierarchy'. There could not have been molecules before there were atoms, nor cells before there were molecules. Babies must learn to sit before they learn to walk and they walk before they run.

It is evident that some things must happen before others become possible. Nevertheless, this axiom is of considerable importance because if we undertake any serious investigation of a process it requires us to establish the order of constituent events. This leads to important discoveries, particularly in the field of education where the events that make up learning and the order in which they must occur are often not identified at a sufficiently detailed level.

*   *   *

These laws and this axiom can be found as easily in a good lesson as in the history of the universe. With this introduction, we are now ready to begin looking at Gattegno's model of evolution.

## An introduction to Gattegno's model of evolution

Gattegno invites us to study all phenomena as manifestations of energy. In his model, which he first presented in 1959, the story of evolution is the story of the evolution of energy, and this begins with the Big Bang rather than with the emergence of life. Gattegno described the process of evolution using a vertical vector to represent significant advances in the economics of energy, and a horizontal vector to represent the on-going exploration of the implications and possibilities that any such advance permits. He describes the nature of energy as being to explore and to create.

## Cosmic energy - the first realm

### Elements

Physicists presently situate the beginning of our universe at the Big Bang, around fourteen billion years ago. Energy first evolved through the creation of new elements. From hydrogen, the simplest atom, helium, lithium and so on were created by a process of what Gattegno called 'complexation', until all the nuclei of the elements known to exist in a natural state had come into existence. (Ninety-two were known when Gattegno was alive.) This was mainly elucidated by physicists during the first half of the twentieth century.

This first type of evolution continues to take place in stars. "I propose this hypothesis: A star is a cosmic laboratory in which energies are transformed into atoms". (1982-1983 vol.I:33) To characterise energy at this stage in its development, Gattegno called it 'cosmic energy': energy which allows its own condensation into matter through processes we do not yet understand.

It might seem that this 'horizontal' evolution could continue indefinitely, with more and more complex elements appearing. But this is not what took place. All further elements begin to disintegrate as soon as they come into existence, as demonstrated in laboratories around the world. Energy can, therefore, no longer continue this type of evolution and finds itself blocked. This is "the first impasse", the end of a horizontal evolution.

## Molecules

The way for evolution to continue is by means of a qualitatively different approach, a 'vertical leap' in Gattegno's terminology. This was the emergence of molecules, from simple assemblies of two atoms that appeared very early on, through to proteins which are made up of whole chains of atoms. Molecules allow energy to engage itself in a new horizontal evolution, very different from the preceding one.

> In the view I am presenting to you here, a view of cosmic energy objectifying itself, the molecule is a new adventure. It is something quite different from the adventure of the atom ... at the atomic level, matter is linked by 'the strong force' in order to create atomic nuclei. Here, cosmic energy expresses itself as two atoms which go towards each other and which attach one to the other electrically. (1982-1983 vol.I:62)

This evolution began with simple linkages but on earth it has also created large molecules comprised of carbon plus a few other atoms, studied in organic chemistry. We find molecules like DNA made up of thousands and thousands of atoms.

Gattegno pointed out that certain features of the first horizontal evolution are also to be found in the evolution of molecules.

Firstly, in molecular evolution the quantities of energy required are considerably less than what was required at the atomic level; much less energy is needed to link two atoms of hydrogen to an atom of oxygen than to create the atoms themselves. This is an example of the law of economy of energy.

Secondly, molecular evolution can take place as long as it is possible to create new molecules which are bigger and bigger, more and more complex, but there comes a time when the molecules are so big that they break down, and evolution finds itself once again in an impasse. What takes place is a new vertical leap.

## Vital energy- the second and third realms

Energy evolved by taking a new form, vital energy, and thus a new way of being, the cell.

The cell introduces a way of maintaining a considerable number of molecules in close proximity on a semi-permanent basis, thus allowing a new range of processes to take place through the interaction of these molecules amongst themselves.

Vital energy gives itself two directions of exploration, the domain of form exemplified by plants which is the second, vegetal realm, and then that of behaviour exemplified by animals, the third realm.

The law of subordination and integration describes the relationship between these realms. Elements are combined to produce molecules in the first realm; both elements and molecules are used by cells in the second realm to produce forms; elements, molecules and forms are used in the third realm in the production of constellations of behaviours. Evolution is a cumulative process.

Each vertical leap allows a new horizontal evolution to unfold.

### The second realm - the realm of cells and plants

One of the descriptions that Gattegno gave of the second or vegetal realm was that, "the universe of plants is the total number of possible attempts at producing forms from molecules." (1982-1983 vol.I:276) Molecules borrowed from the environment are put together to create forms. As botanists recognise, what distinguishes one plant from another and from all others is its form.

In the second realm,

> ... form takes precedence in the manner an electromagnetic field affects the positions, distances, and general configurations of sets of iron filings, without touching the physical or chemical attributes of matter. (1982b XI 5:12)

Two problems must be solved: how to maintain a form over generations, and how a change of form is possible. The first of these is studied in the field of genetics but Gattegno pointed out that form is also maintained through the use of molecules with qualities that are adapted to the form required by a given cell. "If you look at the molecular content of [rectangular or linear bacteria] you will see that they use components which are noticeably straight and long." (1982-1983 vol.I:275)

However, he further argued that something else was needed: vital energy.

> Plants are the realm of cells in which the new form of cosmic energy, called 'vital energy', acts upon molecular energy, not only to make more and new molecules, but also to organize them in space so that this aggregate remain together for some time. A plant takes from the environment the molecules it will keep in its cells, while maintaining its own form as its characteristics. Vital energy is also needed to produce new forms, starting with whatever components are available. (1982b XI 5:12)

For Gattegno, vital energy is a new form of energy which subordinates the previous forms, molecular and cosmic energy, and integrates them. It is the mechanism through which form is actively explored.

> Evolution in the vegetable kingdom is the movement of vital energy from one viable form to another, keeping what works, and experimenting with properties capable of being acted upon, but [which] were not specially involved in the activities of previous species. If the experiment proves that such properties are a province of vital energy, a new plant is generated. If not, there is no trace left behind of that trial. The vegetable kingdom is only made up of the successful experiments of vital energy. Its immense variety can teach us how forms evolve, and how much room vital energy found for its trials upon objectified cosmic energy (atoms and molecules) as well as upon other forms working on the same matter. (1982b XI 5:13)

For Gattegno, "vital energy manifests itself in a great many forms; there is not just one single form of vital energy, just as there is not only one single form of cosmic energy." (1982-1983 vol.II:31)

Just as cosmic energy can exist as chemical energy, gravitational energy, electromagnetic energy, heat or several other forms of energy, so vital energy can exist in the forms of all the plants which exist or have ever existed. For Gattegno (1982-1983 vol.I:301), vital energy is freer than cosmic energy because it can choose the forms it will take.

Among the unsolved problems of biology, Gattegno (1982-1983 vol.II:29) cited the fact that no one yet knew how sap moves up to the top of a tall tree. Atmospheric pressure can take it up 10 metres and capillary tension can move it up another few metres, but something else is necessary if the sap is to climb to heights of 80 metres, as it does in the Giant Sequoias of California. As long as one thinks in terms of mechanics, there was no solution to this problem. But, since the tubes and the capillaries in which the sap climbs are living, one can well imagine that vital energy has devised a mechanism that takes advantages of the properties of living matter.

In this realm as in the cosmic realm, the law of economy of energy is at work. Much less energy is spent in order to hold the plants in their various shapes than is required to keep molecules together. One only needs to separate each into their constituent parts to realize this.

It becomes clear that the effects of evolution are cumulative. Once a solution has been found for any given problem, this solution is retained. Thus, for example, once sexuality appeared at the level of the vegetal realm, it was maintained in the animal and human realms.

Gattegno rejects Darwin's hypothesis of evolution by natural selection in favour of a deliberate exploration of possibilities, since, for him, it is not possible to imagine that the huge variety of plants that we know is the result of chance mutations.

> Almost everyone ... adheres to the Darwinian line. There is an alternative, ... it is that the energies look for all the possible forms and, from these, some are viable, others are not. Or we can say: "those which survive are viable; the others are not." (1982-1983 vol.II:83)

Gattegno (1982-1983 vol.II:75) points to certain plants which send a root down vertically into the soil. If the root encounters an obstacle, it tries to push it aside. If it cannot do so, it tries to dissolve it chemically. If this does not succeed, the root goes off horizontally until it can get around the obstacle. But then, instead of going down vertically from the new position, the root goes back horizontally until it is under its starting place. Only then does it begin going down vertically again. What struggle for survival can explain this?

The conclusion that Gattegno drew from this and other phenomena that would otherwise appear to be anomalous, is that plants demonstrate awareness. Otherwise, such phenomena would not be possible. The awareness demonstrated by plants is not as developed as that shown by human beings or animals, but it is sufficient for what plants have to do in order to survive. Climbing plants have to recognise the existence of a support on which to climb. Plants which adapt their way of living to the seasons must sense changes of temperature and light conditions as they take place. Those which follow the sun must know where the sun is at any given moment.

We should notice that in each realm, there are entities which foreshadow what will be found in the following realm. Thus, in the realm of molecules, viruses exist. These are large molecules which associate themselves with other molecules before breaking up, only to associate themselves anew with still other molecules, a system which foreshadows reproduction. Viruses are the most complex molecules known, but they are not yet living creatures.

### The third realm - the realm of animals
The third realm is that of the exploration of behaviours, expressing a specific energy called instinct. Gattegno proposes that, "each species of animal is an instinct which gave itself its form in order to survive." (1982-1983 vol.II:104)

In the case of animals, vital energy is subordinated to an animal energy, instinct, which integrates it. Animals all have a form, since they are the product of vital energy, but they can impose changes on this form - within certain limits - which are the result of their behaviours. The forms generated are those best adapted for the behaviours of the species.

In the study of the third realm,

> [W]e have ... the difficult task of seeing how vital energy is at the service of instinct, what represents the spectrum of instincts, and how it is possible to understand that so many instincts, so many species, exist; what makes a species change into another, and how we are going

to work on these data in order to describe the whole of animal life. (1982-1983 vol.II:105)

## Instinct

How can one conceive of instinct as energy? In a comparison of unicellular plants and unicellular animals, we see instinct at work. If one studies a bacterium and an amoeba under a microscope, one sees immediately that the amoeba moves out of the field of vision and it is necessary to constantly readjust the microscope in order to see it, while the bacterium stays in place. It is not easy to learn how to move. For Gattegno, we are looking at a new energy at work.

> The amoeba manages to understand, from the point of view of its energy, what it must do to throw ahead a part of itself. It changes shape, as if it had the choice, the right, to put out any part of itself like an advancing foot. (1982-1983 vol.II:112-113)

In other words, the amoeba has a behaviour and this is what distinguishes it from the bacterium.

Instinct is an energy. Clearly it is not the energy the animal consumes in order to live, nor is it the individual animal's 'quantum', which allows each animal to be an individual within its species. Rather, instinct circumscribes the animal's constellation of behaviours. It is more labile than the vital energy of plants, whose action on form is slower to evolve.

The animal quantum, when it frees itself of instinct, will become the self in humans.

Evolution in this realm occurs when an individual quantum of energy, an animal,

> ... requests the instinct to adjust to singular circumstances which may reveal to the quantum a possibility not yet encountered in life. ... By staying with this revelation and its repeated use, the instinct is altered by the objectivation of the new behavior on the pre-existing form. This, in turn, becomes distinctive and second nature. Other individuals of the species who witness this behavior, understanding how their quantum can affect their use of their form, will demonstrate that the boundaries, associated with the initial instinct, can be transcended and a new animal generated. This new animal will form a new species having a distinctive instinct which includes the energizing of the new behavior. Through this instinct the individuals of

this species will separate themselves from those from which they originally stemmed. (1982b:17)

For Gattegno, " ... the evolution of instinct consists in creating the inventory of all behaviours and all the possible constellations of behaviours." (1982-1983 vol.II:116) There will remain all the experiments which are a success; those which are not viable will lead to extinction.

Each constellation of behaviours is characteristic of a species of animal, and each individual belongs to a species if its behaviours fall within that characteristic constellation of behaviours. However the more evolved the animal, the more freedom it displays. Highly evolved animals such as those one sees on the African savannah live quite freely within the constraints of their instinct and can show widely varying behaviours. Any individual animal's behaviours are in harmony with its instinct but are its alone. Hence, it is the individual who has the capacity to evolve rather than the species.

A behaviour is visible from the outside and can be described. It is the job of naturalists to create the inventory of species by giving us the inventory of constellations of behaviours. For example, such and such a type of bird is identical to its neighbour except that it eats insects and not grains; thus it belongs to a different species.

Instinct determines, among other things, what an animal perceives. A lion in a pasture does not see food around it and will die of hunger unless a goat happens to come along. A goat, in a herd of goats, does not perceive the other goats as food and it will die of hunger if it does not find a pasture. Similarly, the perception of what constitutes a danger is determined by instinct. In animals, perception is functional.

### The mechanism of the creation of species
In animal evolution, there is, once again, a considerable reduction in the quantity of energy used to maintain the system. Animals sustain their lives by finding their food around them and this gives them sufficient energy to undertake exploration of the environment. The more advanced the animal is in the scale of species, the greater the gain in energy. This energy can be used for activities which are compatible with the soma of the animal, even if they are outside the usual constellation of behaviours.

Very evolved animals even have free time; time which they use, for example, for play or for the education of their offspring, and also for exploration which can lead them to new discoveries and perhaps to the creation of a new species.

> As soon as one accepts that there is an additional energy, one is in a position to see what is called 'adaptation'; this is the capacity of the animal to enter into contact with contingencies which were not fore-seen in the animal's heredity. (1982-1983 vol.II:188)

In the third realm again, Gattegno rejected Darwin's theory of evolution. He did not consider that the life of an animal could be reduced to just the struggle for survival and the reproduction of the species. To think in those terms is to miss seeing what any one animal does with its time. There is some space between surviving and living one's life, and this is where each individual animal finds a certain liberty of action which allows it to ex-plore and to discover the limits and the frontiers of its instinct. "The life of an animal is to do everything that is compatible with its instinct, not only to survive and reproduce." (1982-1983 vol.II:129-130) For Gattegno, the proliferation of species was not due to an adaptation to the environment, but to individuals who went beyond what their instinct dictated. Individu-als, and not species, are the agents of evolution; when one looks for a mechanism which could allow species to evolve, one sees that it is not pos-sible to conceive of species being the agents of evolution.

Each individual that goes beyond what its instinct dictates can produce a new species because the animal quantum is in direct contact with the soma it gave itself and can modify its genetic structure. The modification of genetic structure does not demand a lot of energy. For random muta-tion, biologists have supposed that radiation is sufficient.

Gattegno rejected the notion that spontaneous and externally induced changes to DNA cause the mutation of species, because he did not believe that the immense variety one can see in animals can be the fruit of sheer chance. Instead, he argued that the energy necessary to effect these changes is very, very small, and that an animal can mobilise enough ener-gy to produce them at will. The creation of a new species is willed by the animal quantum which lives the adventure of finding itself suddenly out-side its instinct and which modifies its DNA on the molecular level to perpetuate itself.

One cannot fail to be struck by the fact that the soma of animals is always so perfectly adapted to the expression of the instinct of the species. The law of subordination and integration functions here too. Instinct inte-grates the vital energy of form, the previous realm, while subordinating it.

Instinct is present in the first cell, and works at the level of the energies of the cell. "The soma is the expression of the instinct." (1982-1983 vol.II:197) Instinct is not simply added to the animal once it is formed. When one conceives of an animal as an energy manifesting itself as a constellation of behaviours giving itself a form suited to expressing them, one can understand how the energy of the instinct can produce an appropriate form.

The energies present are in a hierarchy. Instinct integrates vital energy which integrates the cosmic energy present in the molecules - for the animal is also of the first and second realms.

> It is possible to change the form because instinct has taken command of vital energy; instinct uses vital energy automatically, just as vital energy uses molecules automatically. (1982-1983 vol.II:139)

In this way, "we place permanence, maintenance, continuation in the genetic system; we see variation in the instinct, there we see what can create something different." (1982-1983 vol.II:204)

## The attributes of animals

Gattegno grants animals an awareness. "Two sheep know they are themselves and not 'that one is the other'; it is the same for two ants or two lice because if one eats, the other is not satiated!" (1982-1983 vol.II:153)

Each animal knows when it is hungry. It is aware of its hunger, of the fact that it looks for food, that it eats and that it is no longer hungry. It is not necessary for this awareness to be very developed for us to accept that it exists. It exists in all animals, whatever their stage of evolution, and it is necessary and sufficient for the survival of the animal.

Similarly, Gattegno grants animals a sense of time and a will; they prove this when they wait patiently in front of a hole until their prey comes out, and also when they mobilise themselves to seize it and when they leap. These acts - the act of not leaping as well as that of leaping - require the same mobilisation as similar acts in human beings.

## Genetics and the role of DNA

Gattegno's model does not deny a role to DNA, which gives a spider what it needs to be a web maker. However, DNA cannot show *this* spider how to weave *this* web around *this* nail in *this* corner of *this* wall. The spider must have enough awareness to be able to do so. DNA makes available billions of years of evolution, putting them at the service of each living creature at the beginning of its life as an individual. But each creature lives its life with an awareness sufficient for its needs.

Heredity by the transmission of genes from one generation to another is not in doubt. But it has never been proved that this is the only way of transmitting information from one generation to another.

Now that animals have managed to inhabit an astounding variety of ecological niches over the surface of the earth, the way for energy to evolve further is for it to make another vertical leap, to create a new realm, that of humans.

| Realm | Vertical leap | Horizontal evolution |
|---|---|---|
| First or cosmic realm | Atomic energy | Elements |
| | Molecular energy | Molecules |
| Second or vegetal realm | Vital energy | Forms |
| Third or animal realm | Animal energy ("vital energy with a twist") | Instinct |
| Fourth or human realm | Human energy | Self |

## The fourth realm - human beings

[A]n understanding of evolution in humans cannot be an extension of that which has been acceptable for plants and animals. (1982b:10)

Human beings create a realm by becoming aware that one does not have to live within an instinct as animals do. Humans have no instinct and are not limited to any particular constellation of behaviours. They can choose their behaviours and change them at will, as many times as they want to during a lifetime. They can choose to reproduce or not, to be vegetarians, fruit eaters or omnivores; to live in the desert or on the plains... They are singularly free to live as they decide, even if they choose to remain within a culture that appears to determine many of their behaviours. For this reason, it follows that each human is a species in his own right, since each person's behaviours are idiosyncratic and unique to him.

There are as many species of humans as there are humans.

> The passage to humanity took place the day one of these animals ...
> recognized itself as an energy which was not instinctual; he identified
> with his free energy and the relation with his soma was no longer: "I
> gave myself a soma to represent my behaviours," but: "I have an en-
> ergy at my disposition which allows me to use this soma to create
> behaviours." And thus, we are compelled to say that each individual
> is a species. (1982-1983 vol.II:271)

Gattegno calls the free energy mentioned above 'the self'. Once the self
comes into existence, behaviours continue to exist but they appear
through culture, learning and choice rather than through heredity;
humans can change their behaviours at will.

> All evolution has first taken place in individuals and, when possible,
> [been] passed on to others by various means of heredity. In humans,
> however, there are only individuals. Thus, evolution simply means
> experimenting with awareness individually, deciding whether to af-
> fect or not to affect all one's life by the transfer of what one has
> managed to become aware of. Thus evolution (i.e. conscious evolu-
> tion) is deliberate only in the fourth realm. (1982b:10)

From the massive amounts of energy involved in the earliest stage of evolution, Gattegno saw a progressive increase in yield with each vertical leap
– more for less - to the point where the energy of the fourth realm is that
of awareness and costs no more than human thought. Because awarenesses require so little energy, Gattegno sometimes called them 'nothings'.

> [Man] can polarize his mind so that when working on energy he sees
> 'energy' as 'energies', the plural which indicates a deeper and more
> varied approach to a recently discovered entity (about 100 years old)
> whose presence in men's minds has transformed his outer and inner
> environments. This deeper approach may lead him to see the whole
> of evolution as the story of the evolution of energy over time, allow-
> ing successive increases in yield to result from smaller expenditures
> (a clear economic viewpoint) ending with 'the dynamics of nothings',
> seen as the present day stage of that enquiry. (1984 XIII 3:5)

There has been a similar gain in time:

> It was necessary to use cosmic lengths of time to do the jobs which
> involved:
>
> 1.    atomic or molecular changes;

2. an expansion of the working of form to test viability;

3. an alteration in sets of behaviors by adding a new one and then testing viability with it.

However, such lengths of time are no longer needed on earth to feed back to humans that a human proposal (e.g. to use human energy to starve a behavior or enhance it) is open to all. In one life it is possible to know, sometimes in a few minutes, whether or not that which comes to one's mind is compatible with the then prevailing conditions. From such feedback, one can decide whether or not to remain in contact with that which was being contemplated. (1982b:20)

Gattegno was fond of saying to teachers who might be tempted to underestimate their students, that all human beings are at the summit of thirteen billion years of evolution, in which Nature has only kept what was successful.

## Further reading

*L'énergie et les énergies* (especially Volume III which gives a detailed study of human beings)

Energy, time, evolutionary impasses and man – *Newsletter XI.5*

A reconsideration of the sciences – *Newsletter XIV.4*

# Appendices

# A  On consciousness

People sometimes ask why the words 'conscious' and 'consciousness' are not used in Gattegno's model and only rarely appear in his books. As far as we know, he himself did not explain why he did not use these words. However, we can make the following observations:

1        He did, in fact, use the words in his early work in English. They gave way to 'presence', 'awareness' and 'awarenesses'; the last being used to describe the discrete movements of the mind, moment by moment, that he observed in himself and others.

2        He did his early work on this aspect of the model in French, where there is no distinction between words for 'awareness' and 'consciousness', both being translated by *la conscience*. The translation of 'an awareness' in French is *une prise de conscience* (a 'gelling' of awareness, from a sense of *prise* that also exists in English when one talks about jelly or concrete 'taking', and perhaps when one talks about making a 'mis-take').

3        The words 'conscious' and 'consciousness' do not lend themselves to becoming countable nouns suitable to translate *une prise de conscience*. Gattegno must have realised that the word 'awareness', on the other hand, could be adapted to this end. The idea of 'an awareness' shocks in English until one recognises awarenesses in oneself, at which point it becomes indispensable.

4        'Consciousness' already carries a number of connotations, few of them precise. By coining the notion of 'an awareness' Gattegno gave himself the freedom to define it.

5        He seems to use 'consciousness', at least on some occasions, to describe awareness when there is also some simultaneous awareness of the self that knows.

6        'Consciousness' also seems less suitable for his purposes than 'awareness' because it typically connotes a greater extension in time. Thus

it is more suitable for descriptions of activities like contemplation and less suitable for descriptions of small, fast movements of the mind.

7        When he described memories, he liked to use 'consciousness'; ie memories being "triggered into consciousness", "evoked into consciousness", etc.

8        In a physiological use of the word, 'consciousness' is opposed to 'unconsciousness', which is considered a loss of presence to both the outer and inner worlds, for example, during sleep. Gattegno's model rejects the notion that we are unconscious during sleep, instead proposing that the self has two states of being, the waking state and the sleeping state, as described in Chapter 3. The self is highly active during sleep.

9        In the field of psychoanalysis, models have been developed which posit unconscious operations of the mind. Gattegno's model views these as the result of activity taking place between the self and the psyche.

10       One view of consciousness equates it with the capacity to make a verbal report. In Gattegno's model the self is present in the first cell, and is aware. If consciousness can only exist with language, then clearly the word is unsuitable for Gattegno's purposes.

# B   The psyche as an energy

One of us (PM) has difficulty with the idea that the psyche is an energy.

If we understand the soma as encompassing all the physical material within the bag then the material of the nervous system and brain are part of the soma. But the functions of the psyche would seem to be at least partly the result of the arrangement and interconnections between the cells of this tissue, what is sometimes called the 'soft-wiring'. This configuration of matter certainly required energy to put it into place (so it is the result or, perhaps, 'residue' of energy spent), but it seems harder to say that the configuration per se is now energy unless information can be conceived of as energy.

Gattegno (1985:9) said something which might bear on this. It seems that he was prepared to see 'forces' as a form that energy takes:

> No one doubts that energy, met in the world at large and in social instances, can have several forms. Since they are interchangeable, a ready concept can take care of it all: there is only one energy — that studied by physicists — and it has not quite a dozen forms: potential, kinetic, heat, chemical, electrostatic, magnetic, electrodynamic and electromagnetic, radiation, gravitational.

> But cosmologists, nuclear physicists, and perhaps philosophers among them, see four energies in their worlds: the gravitational, the electromagnetic, and the weak and strong forces of atomic physics. These are not the same distinctions as those of the above paragraphs. They are looked at as quantitatively interchangeable like those, but they are examined both for their qualitative differences, and for the fact that scientists are unable to unify them. Scientists cannot quite believe that there may be essential differences which might force us to admit that a number of energies exist, and they continue trying to unify the four. They are aware of their belief, but not yet that it is a belief.

There have been proposals from others that we should see information as energy. If our sense of energy is broadened from the original sense in which it was used in classical physics, then Gattegno's description of psyche as energy seems acceptable.

# C  Selected bibliography for Caleb Gattegno

For a full bibliography of works by Gattegno, see the Educational Solutions or Cuisenaire Company website.

Publishers :

| | |
|---|---|
| CLIL | Center for Language and Intercultural Learning, Osaka |
| D&N | Delachaux & Niestlé, Neuchâtel and Paris |
| DBD | David B. Davies |
| EdExp | Educational Explorers, Reading |
| EdSols | Educational Solutions, New York |
| O&D | Outerbridge & Dienstfrey, New York |
| RKP | Routledge & Kegan Paul, London |
| UEcPD | Une Ecole Pour Demain, Lyons |
| UEPD | Une Education Pour Demain, Besançon |

| | |
|---|---|
| 1952 | *Introduction à la psychologie de l'affectivité et à l'éducation à l'amour*, D&N, translated into English as *The Adolescent and his Self* |
| 1960 | *Now Johnny Can Do Arithmetic*, EdExp, translated into French as *Enfin, Freddy comprend l'arithmétique* |
| 1961 | *Arithmetic with Numbers in Colour*, Books 7, 8 and 9, EdExp |
| 1962 | *Mathematics with Numbers in Colour*, EdExp |
| 1962 | *The Adolescent and his Self*, EdExp |
| 1963 | *Teaching Foreign Languages in Schools*, EdExp. Second edition 1972, EdSols |
| 1966 | *Mathématiques avec les nombres en couleurs*, D&N |
| 1967 | *Conscience de la conscience*, D&N |
| 1969 | *Reading with Words in Colour*, EdExp |
| 1969 | *Towards a Visual Culture*, O&D, published in French as *Vers une culture visuelle* |
| 1971 | *What We Owe Children: The Subordination of Teaching to Learning*, RKP |
| 1971 | *Geoboard Geometry*, EdSols |

1972     *Ces enfants nos maîtres: la subordination de l'enseignement à l'apprentissage*, D&N, French translation of *What We Owe Children*

1973     *In the Beginning there were no Words: The Universe of Babies*, EdSols

1974     *The Common Sense of Teaching Mathematics*, EdSols

1975     *Of Boys and Girls*, EdSols

1975     *On Being Freer*, EdSols

1975     *The Mind Teaches the Brain*, EdSols

1976     *Le cerveau*, UEcPD

1976     *The Common Sense of Teaching Foreign Languages*, EdSols

1977     *Evolution and Memory*, EdSols

1977     *On Love*, EdSols

1977     *Awareness of the Awareness*, Chapter 2 of *The Science of Education*, 1987, EdSols

1977     *The Facts of Awareness*, Chapter 3 of *The Science of Education*, 1987, EdSols

1977     *Affectivity and Learning*, Chapter 4 of *The Science of Education*, 1987, EdSols

1978     *De l'intuition*, UEcPD

1978     *On Death: an essay*, EdSols

1978     *De l'affectivité*, UEcPD

1979     *English the Silent Way, a Video Program*, EdSols

1979     *Du temps*, UEcPD (four volumes)

1979     *Who Cares about Health?* EdSols

1982     Thirty Years Later *Mathematics Teaching* 100

1982     *L'énergie et les énergies*, UEcPD (three volumes)

1984     *Ma mort*, UEcPD

1985     *The Common Sense of Teaching Reading and Writing*, EdSols

1985     *The Learning and Teaching of Foreign Languages*, Chapter 13 of *The Science of Education*, EdSols

1985     *De L1 à L2*, UEPD

1985     *Les forces psychiques qui nous aident*, UEPD

1986     *L'univers des bébés*, translation of *In the beginning there were no words: The Universe of Babies*, UEPD

1986     *La génération des richesses*, UEPD (two volumes)

1986     *The Generation of Wealth*, EdSols

1986     *Memory and Retention*, Chapter 5 of The Science of Education

1987     *The Science of Education, Part 1, Theoretical Considerations*, EdSols,

1987     *La psychologie des petits enfants*, UEPD

1987     *Peut-on changer son passé ?* UEPD

1987     *Une théorie générale de la relativité humaine*, UEPD

1987     *L'amour*, UEPD

1987     *Etre libre*, UEPD

1988     *Know Your Children as They Are: a Book for Parents*, EdSols

1988    *Peut-on penser en termes positifs à l'avenir de nos enfants ?* UEPD
1988    *Les disciplines spirituelles qui nous aident à vivre à être heureux,* UEPD
1988    *La lecture en couleurs,* UEPD

## Books and seminars published posthumously

1989    *The Science of Education, Part 2, The Mathematisation of Awareness,* EdSols
1989    *Connaître ses enfants tels qu'ils sont,* French translation of *Know Your Children as They Are: a Book for Parents,* UEPD
1989    *La créativité,* UEPD
1989    *Awareness for Teaching and for Research on Teaching,* DBD
1990    *Les mathématiques,* UEPD
1990    *Can I be Creative?* DBD
1990    *Les mystères de la communication,* UEPD
1991    *The History of Mathematics in Terms of Awareness,* DBD
1992    *La mémoire,* UEPD
1992    *Vivre à son sommet,* UEPD
1993    *Y a-t-il des raisons d'être optimiste à la fin du vingtième siècle?* UEPD
1993    *The Science of Education,* CLIL
1994    *A-t-on le droit de ne pas être pessimiste?* UEPD
1995    *A la recherche de ma place,* UEPD
1996    *De la santé,* UEPD
1996    *Awareness,* DBD
1997    *L'expérience collective au service des individus,* UEPD
2011    *La science de l'éducation, tomes 1 et 2, chapitre 13,* translation of *The Science of Education,* all parts, UEPD

## Newsletters

| | | |
|---|---|---|
| Educational Solutions | II.2 | January 1973 |
| Mathematics | II.3 | March 1973 |
| Bilingualism | II.4 | April 1973 |
| Reading | II.5 | June 1973 |
| | | |
| The Silent Way | III.4 | April 1974 |
| Thoughts for the Summer | III.5 | June 1974 |
| | | |
| Our Work in Remediation | IV.1 | September 1974 |
| ESL, The Silent Way | IV.3 | February 1975 |
| On Early Childhood | IV.4 | April 1975 |
| Affectivity and Learning | IV.5 | June 1975 |

| | | |
|---|---|---|
| Energy, Time, Evolutionary Impasses and Man | XI .5 | June 1982 |
| The Origin and Evolution of Language | XII.1 | September 1982 |
| Transfer of Learning | XII.2 | December 1982 |
| The Economics of Education – an Alternative View | XII.3 | February 1983 |
| Time: Public and Private | XII.4 | April 1983 |
| Looking Back and Then Forward | XII.5 | June 1983 |
| Making Silent Way Materials - An Invitation for Teamwork | XIII.1 | September 1983 |
| The Need to Know | XIII.2 | December 1983 |
| Homo Economicus | XIII.3 | February 1984 |
| Man Must Experiment | XIII.4 | April 1984 |
| Whence Morality? | XIII.5 | June 1984 |
| Understanding Disagreements | XIV.1 | September 1984 |
| The Powers of Self-Education Maintained | XIV.2 | December 1984 |
| What's a Good Question? | XIV.3 | February 1985 |
| A Reconsideration of the Sciences | XIV.4 | April 1985 |
| The Silent Way and Zen | XIV.5 | June 1985 |
| What is Man? | XV.1-2 | Sept/Dec 1985 |
| Sleep Revisited | XV.3-4 | February/April 1986 |
| Can Language Teachers be Open-Minded? | XV.5 | June 1986 |
| Collective Experiments | XVI.1 | September 1986 |
| A Working Model for Health | XVI.2-4 | Dec/Feb/April1987 |
| Caleb Gattegno's Achievements | XVI.5 | June 1987 |
| From Pre-Humanity to Humanity | XVII.1 | September 1987 |
| Education and the Present World Crisis | XVII.2 | December 1987 |
| Of Music and Language | XVII.3 | February 1988 |
| The Hebrew-Jewish Experiment | XVII.4-5 | April/June 1988 |

**Books published as a joint author**

1952    Gattegno, Caleb and Alphonse Gay, *Un nouveau phénomène psychosomatique*, D&N

1960    Cuisenaire, Georges and Caleb Gattegno, *Initiation à la méthode: les nombres en couleurs*, D&N. Second edition as *Initiation aux nombres en couleurs*, D&N

1949    Ostrowski, Alexander and Caleb Gattegno, *Representation confornales ? à la frontière*, Gauthiers –Villars (other details unknown)

### Translations into English

1951    Gattegno, C. and F. M. Hodgson *Play, Dreams and Imitation* by Jean Piaget, RKP

1951    Gattegno, C. and F. M. Hodgson *The Child's Concept of Number* by Jean Piaget, RKP

### Translations into French

1949    Gattegno, C. *Polynômes de base* by J. M. Whittaker (other details unknown)

### Series edited by Caleb Gattegno

1964    More than 50 titles in the series *My Life and My Work* (descriptions of professions written by professionals), EdExp

### Software published by Educational Solutions, New York

1. The Infused Reading Series
1982    Lectura Infusa in Spanish
1983    La lecture Infuse in French
1984    Infused Reading in Iñupiaq
1985    Infused Reading in Ojibwe
1986    Lettura Infusa in Italian
1986    Infused Reading in Lacotan
1986    Das eigeniesses lesen für Deutsch
1986    Infused Reading in English
1987    Infused Reading in Hawaiian
1987    Infused Reading in Maori
1987    Infused Reading in Samoan
1987    Infused Reading in Tahitian

2. Spelling in English
1986    Writing English: a Study of Spelling

3. Mathematics

| 1981 | Visible and Tangible Math 1 | Numeration up to 1000 |
| 1981 | Visible and Tangible Math 2 | Thousands |
| 1981 | Visible and Tangible Math 2A | Pyramid Games |
| 1981 | Visible and Tangible Math 3 | Counting |
| 1981 | Visible and Tangible Math 4 | Complementarity |
| 1981 | Visible and Tangible Math 5 | Complements |
| 1981 | Visible and Tangible Math 6 | From Number Pairs to Operations |
| 1981 | Visible and Tangible Math 6A | From Number Pairs to Operations 2 |
| 1981 | Visible and Tangible Math 7 | Classes of Equivalence |
| 1981 | Visible and Tangible Math 8 | Transformations |
| 1981 | Visible and Tangible Math 9 | Addition & Subtraction by Transformations |
| 1981 | Visible and Tangible Math 10 | Addition & Subtraction in all Bases of Numeration |
| 1985 | Visible and Tangible Math 11 | Multiplication |
| 1986 | Visible and Tangible Math 12 | Multiplication & Division Algorithm |

**Films published by Educational Solutions, New York**

| 1970 | Pop ups: 18 one-minute sequences for learning to read in English |
| 1972 | Pop ups: 37 one-minute sequences for learning to read in Spanish |
| 1974 | Absolute Visual Reading (for the deaf) |
| 1977 | Animated Geometry, The Family of Circles |
| 1977 | Animated Geometry, The Right Strophoid |
| 1977 | Animated Geometry, The Generation of Conics |
| 1977 | Animated Geometry, Pole and Polars |
| 1977 | Animated Geometry, Circles and Points |
| 1979 | Animated Geometry, Epicycloids and Hypocycloids |
| 1979 | The Foundations of Geometry |

**Video cassettes published by Educational Solutions, New York**

| 1978 | *Silent Way Video Course - English the Silent Way*, 140 lessons in English |
| 1978 | *Silent Way Video Course - Hebrew the Silent Way*, 40 lessons in Hebrew |

# References

Unless noted, books and newsletters by Caleb Gattegno were originally published by Educational Solutions Inc. in New York. Newsletters are referenced below by their date, volume and issue number (e.g. 1982 XII.1).

Both books and newsletters have now been republished by Educational Solutions Worldwide Inc. in Toronto with new pagination. Page numbers in this book are from the original publications. The new editions can be read free of charge at www.educationalsolutions.com

| 1967 | *Conscience de la conscience.* Neuchâtel: Delachaux & Niestlé |
| 1971 | *What We Owe Children* |
| 1973 | *In the Beginning there were no Words: the Universe of Babies* |
| 1975a | *On Being Freer* |
| 1975b | *Of Boys and Girls* |
| 1975c V.1 | Intuition and complexity |
| 1976 V.5 | On knowledge |
| 1977a | *Evolution and Memory* |
| 1977b | *On Love* |
| 1978a | *On Death* |
| 1978b | *De l'affectivité* (seminar) |
| 1979 VIII.4 | The year of the child: the elementary school years |
| 1979 IX.2 | Knowing: epistemology or psychology |
| 1982-1983 | *L'énergie et les énergies* (seminar, 3 volumes) |

1982a          30 years later, *Mathematics Teaching* Vol 100 (reprinted in *A Gattegno Anthology.* Derby: Association of Teachers of Mathematics)

1982b XI.5     Energy, time, evolutionary impasses and man

1983 XII.4     Time, public and private

1983 XIII.2    The need to know

1984 XIII.3    Homo Economicus

1985           *The Science of Education Chapter 13: The Learning and Teaching of Foreign Languages*

1985 XIV.4     A reconsideration of the sciences

1986 XV.3-4    Sleep revisited

1986 XVI.2-4 A working model for health

1987a          *The Science of Education Part 1: Theoretical Considerations*

1987b          *Can I be creative?* (seminar)

1988a          *The Mind Teaches the Brain* (revised from 1975)

1988b          *Know Your Children as They Are*


Holt, J. (1984) *How Children Fail (revised edition).* London: Pelican Books

Liley, A.W. (1972) The Foetus as a Personality, *Australian and New Zealand Journal of Psychiatry* Vol 6: 99

Marcault, J.-E. & Brosse, T. (1939) *L'éducation de demain.* Paris: Alcan

Scheibel, A.B. (1997) Embryological Development of the Human Brain at http://education.jhu.edu/newhorizons/Neurosciences/articles

Stevick, E.W. (1990) *Humanism in Language Teaching: A Critical Perspective.* OUP

Wolpert, D.M., Ghahramani Z. and Flanagan, J.R. (2001) Perspectives and problems in motor learning, *Trends in Cognitive Sciences* Vol 5 Number 11

www.ingramcontent.com/pod-product-compliance
Lightning Source LLC
Chambersburg PA
CBHW071349280326
41927CB00040B/2523